The Dublin Cattle Market's

Maynooth Studies in Local History

SERIES EDITOR Raymond Gillespie

This volume is one of five short books published in the Maynooth Studies in Local History series in 2021. Like their predecessors they range widely over the local experience in the Irish past. Chronologically they range across the 19th century and into the 20th century but they focus on problems that reappeared in almost every period of Irish history. They chronicle the experiences of individuals grappling with their world from the Cork surgeon, Denis Brenan Bullen, in the early 19th century to the politician and GAA administrator Peadar Cowan in the 20th century. From a different perspective they resurrect whole societies under stress from the rural tensions in Knock, Co. Mayo, to the impact of the Famine on Sir William Palmer's estates in Mayo. A rather different sort of institution under stress, Dublin's cattle market, provides the framework for charting the final years of the world that depended on that institution. Geographically they range across the length of the country from Dublin to Cork and westwards into Mayo. Socially they move from those living on the margins of society in Knock through to the prosperous world of the social elite in Cork. In doing so they reveal diverse and complicated societies that created the local past and present the range of possibilities open to anyone interested in studying that past. Those possibilities involve the dissection of the local experience in the complex and contested social worlds of which it is part as people strove to preserve and enhance their positions within their local societies. It also reveals the forces that made for cohesion in local communities and those that drove people apart, whether through large scale rebellion or through acts of inter-personal violence. Such studies of local worlds over such long periods are vital for the future since they not only stretch the historical imagination but provide a longer perspective on the evolution of society in Ireland and help us to understand more fully the complex evolution of the Irish experience. These works do not simply chronicle events relating to an area within administrative or geographically determined boundaries, but open the possibility of understanding how and why particular regions had their own personality in the past. Such an exercise is clearly one of the most exciting challenges for the future and demonstrates the vitality of the study of local history in Ireland.

Like their predecessors, these five short books are reconstructions of the socially diverse worlds of the poor as well as the rich, women as well as men, the geographical marginal of Mayo as well as those located near the centre of power. They reconstruct the way in which those who inhabited those worlds lived their daily lives, often little affected by the large themes that dominate the writing of national history. In addressing these issues, studies such as those presented in these short books, together with their predecessors, are at the forefront of Irish historical research and represent some of the most innovative and exciting work being undertaken in Irish history today. They also provide models that others can follow up and adapt in their own studies of the Irish past. In such ways will we understand better the regional diversity of Ireland and the social and cultural basis for that diversity. They, with their predecessors, convey the vibrancy and excitement of the world of Irish local history today.

Maynooth Studies in Local History: Number 153

The Dublin Cattle Market's decline, 1955–73
A story of radical change in the Irish livestock industry

Declan O'Brien

FOUR COURTS PRESS

Set in 10pt on 12pt Bembo by
Carrigboy Typesetting Services for
FOUR COURTS PRESS LTD
7 Malpas Street, Dublin 8, Ireland
www.fourcourtspress.ie
and in North America for
FOUR COURTS PRESS
c/o IPG, 814 N Franklin St, Chicago, IL 60610

ISBN 978–1–84682–972–7

Printed in Ireland
by SprintPrint, Dublin.

Contents

FIGURES

Cover photograph, Dublin Cattle Market sale.
All photographs courtesy of Irish Photo Archive, with the exception of figure 3 which was supplied by Martin Ryan.

Acknowledgments

I would like to sincerely thank the people who were interviewed for this study. Jimmy Cosgrave, Joe Barry, Kathleen Donlon and her late husband Jack, Gerard O'Kelly, John Shirley, Maurice Colbert and the late Raymond Keogh were more than generous with their time, advice and knowledge. Likewise, míle buíochas to my late father, Micheál O'Brien. He had such a store of yarns and tales about driving cattle to and from fairs in Limerick during the 1940s and 1950s that I could have written a study on his stories alone. I would like to thank the lecturers and staff at Mary Immaculate College's History Department for their encouragement and advice over the years. It was always appreciated. Similarly, sincere thanks to all in the Research and Graduate School Office in Mary Immaculate College for their help and support. My MA and PhD supervisor, Dr Maura Cronin, deserves a special mention for her support, direction and guidance. It was a pleasure to work with her. Thanks also to Professor Raymond Gillespie and NUI Maynooth for the opportunity to publish this study. Finally, this book would not have been possible without the love and support of my wife, Martina, and the patience of our own Millie.

Introduction: Dublin's cattle masters

The sight of thousands of cattle being driven on foot through the city centre would be unthinkable to most 21st-century Dubliners. However, it was a weekly occurrence up to the 1960s when the capital and the Dublin Cattle Market was the nerve centre of the nation's livestock trade. At its peak in the 1950s the market was among the largest weekly city-based livestock sales in Europe. Located between Phibsboro and the Liffey quays, in an area bordered by Prussia Street, Aughrim Street and St Joseph's Road, the Dublin Cattle Market was held each Wednesday and attracted buyers not only from abattoirs around the city but also British livestock traders acting for slaughter houses and farmers in the north of England.[1] Cattle prices in the Dublin sales centre ebbed and flowed according to the vagaries of the live trade to Britain and the Continent, but the market prospered into the second half of the 20th century and was an established institution in the livestock sector up to the late 1960s.[2] Indeed, at a time when the country's economy depended on agriculture, and the cattle trade in particular, Dublin's market was akin to the national 'stock exchange' – effectively setting prices at fairs and markets throughout the country as dealers based the value of livestock on reports from the Prussia Street sales that were carried on RTÉ radio and in the national newspapers.[3] However, radical changes in the cattle and sheep trade undermined the market's importance and relevance during the 1960s, and by 1973 the Dublin Cattle Market was closed.[4]

This study examines the final years of the Dublin Cattle Market between 1955 and 1973 and assesses the extent to which its demise reflected the radical changes that were taking hold in the Irish livestock industry and in Irish farming generally during this period. Using oral history and documentary evidence, this book will trace the decline of the market as the traditional livestock fairs were eclipsed by the marts, and the live export of cattle to England and Scotland – the cornerstone of the market's business – came under pressure from expanding local slaughtering concerns and government policies that sought to foster and promote the meat-processing industry. This work also explores how the market itself, and particularly the changes that occurred in it through the 1960s, exposed and highlighted tensions within the farming community. These included differences between dealers and farmers, small holders and the large graziers, and dairy farmers and beef finishers. The market was a very rural enterprise in an urban setting. This meeting of the city and country is in itself interesting and the study examines how this dynamic played out at a practical level. Most of those involved in moving livestock around the market were inner

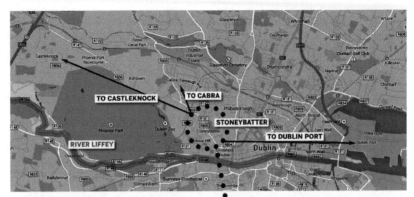

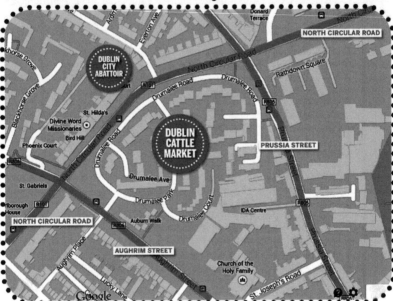

1. The Dublin Cattle Market was located in the north of the city between the North Circular Road and Prussia Street.

city Dubliners, even though their roles could essentially be defined as 'farmers' work'. Using oral evidence and documented interviews with both drovers and the market-stand owners, or sales-masters, who employed them, the book outlines their shared and conflicting memories of the market. Other themes identified in the interviews include family, class and status, as well as urban/rural interaction and a noticeable undercurrent of gender.

Just one historical paper has been written on the market. 'The rise and demise of the Dublin Cattle Market' by Liam Clare was first published in the *Dublin*

Historical Record in 2002. There have been two other books that have dealt with the Dublin Cattle Market in the context of their wider farming operations; these were *Cattleman* by Raymond Keogh and *Strong farmer* by Ciaran Buckley and Chris Ward. However, this new study differs from these publications in that it is based to a large degree on oral testimony. In addition, it focuses on the decline and closure of the market, and asks why it was unable to respond to the challenge posed by the co-operative livestock marts and the emergence of the beef-processing industry. Moreover, it explores what the Dublin Cattle Market's closure said of the standing of agriculture in the economy as Ireland entered the EEC. In addition, the book examines urban/rural relations in the context of the market.

Much of the primary source material for this work comes from oral testimonies, as well as documentary records and photographs. This research formed the basis of the author's MA dissertation; however, it has been supplemented for this book by subsequent work undertaken for a PhD. Those interviewed include three men whose families were sales-masters, Joe Barry, Jimmy Cosgrave and Raymond Keogh. The sales-masters were livestock auctioneers who had stands in the market. These handled the trade in cattle and sheep.[5] The sales-masters sourced cattle at fairs or directly from farmers. They also used agents or local cattle dealers to purchase stock for them. In addition, sales-masters sometimes sold livestock in the market directly for farmers. Sales-masters were essentially livestock traders who were also stand-holders in the Dublin Cattle Market. The interviews with the sales-masters outlined how the market worked. In short, where the cattle were sourced, how they were transported, where they were held in the run-up to the market, and how the animals were sold. The sales-masters also outlined who the primary buyers were, and what type of stock they bought. Moreover, they offered interesting insights into the interactions between the various groups and individuals in the market, and, by extension, on the wider farming sector and on society as a whole. Three farmers were interviewed: Micheál O'Brien and Jack and Kathleen Donlon. The interview with Limerick farmer Micheál O'Brien is relatively short but its significance lies in the fact that it illustrates the national importance of the Dublin Cattle Market by confirming that it helped set the price of cattle in the mid-west. Jack Donlon's account of the livestock trade in the 1960s was important at a number of levels. A retired farmer and cattle trader from Longford, the contributions of Jack and his wife Kathleen were vital because they articulate the views of an intermediary between the farmers and sales-masters. Jack Donlon classed himself as a small-time livestock dealer. He bought cattle from farmers to sell in the market, and, similarly, he purchased livestock in the Dublin market that he later sold to farmers. He was, therefore, ideally placed to comment on the trade overall. The interview with Gerard O'Kelly provided a butcher's perspective on the market. His father owned a butcher's shop at Dolphin's Barn in Dublin and bought cattle and sheep in the market for close to forty years. Gerard O'Kelly's interview outlined how butchers used to buy from particular sales-masters each week, and the importance of these relationships for both parties. The final interviewees were Maurice Colbert, a former senior executive with the Irish Co-operative Organisation Society (ICOS) – the national representative body of the co-operative movement – and retired agricultural journalist John Shirley. Both offered a broader perspective on the establishment of the livestock mart network in the late 1950s and early 1960s, and also on the emergence of the meat processors from the mid-1960s.

In his book on Stoneybatter in Dublin's north inner-city, Kevin Kearns cites four advantages of oral history:

> First, there can be no question as to the correct source. Second, oral histories possess a unique directness and spontaneity. Third, oral interviews typically reveal personal details of life not commonly recorded in written form. Fourth, and perhaps most important, oral history captures and preserves the life experiences of the individuals who lack the time or the literary capability to record their own memories.[6]

In essence, Kearns is describing oral history as a history of ordinary people, and this sentiment tallies with those expressed in the introduction of the second edition of *The oral history reader*.

> While interviews with members of social and political elites have complimented existing documentary sources, the most distinctive contribution of oral history has been to include within the historical record the experiences and perspectives of groups of people who might otherwise have been 'hidden from history'.[7]

The oral history approach certainly offered advantages in this study of Dublin Cattle Market since there were limited documentary sources available. In addition, there was a sense among some who had worked in the market that their numbers were ageing and dwindling and their stories, memories and recollections of the market would be lost if they were not recorded and documented.

Kearns writes of the benefits of interviewing people in their own homes as it is conducive to 'easy rapport and natural conversation', and this was certainly the case with regard to the Dublin Cattle Market interviews.[8] All of the participants, with the exception of Maurice Colbert, were interviewed in their own homes. Maurice and John Shirley chose to be interviewed together, and that took place in John's home. Jack and Kathleen Donlon were also interviewed together. While Hugo Slim, Paul Thompson, Olivia Bennett and Nigel Cross cautioned of possible demerits of group interviews, the experience for this study was very positive in both instances. Slim and his co-authors suggest that:

A group may subtly pressurise people towards a socially acceptable testimony or a mythical representation of the past, or of a current issue which everyone feels is 'safe' and which may be in some sense idealized.[9]

However, in contrast, during both interviews the parties actually reminded one another of events and this often encouraged a more in-depth analysis of the issues raised. At no stage in either interview did any one of the four people seek to limit the discussion in any way. As with Maura Cronin's work on the creameries, most of those contacted about doing an interview for this research reacted positively.[10] What the process entailed was discussed with most of the interviewees prior to the actual interview, and in some cases sample questions were forwarded beforehand and the likely areas for discussion outlined. The interview approach employed was that set out by Hugo Slim, Paul Thompson, Olivia Bennett and Nigel Cross in their essay 'Ways of listening' – the subject was allowed to speak without interruption and the questions were generally short and to the point.[11] This occasionally resulted in rambling replies, which made transcribing some interviews rather difficult. Indeed, Allesandro Portelli's observations on interfering with the spoken word came to mind during this process.

Punctuation indicates pauses distributed according to grammatical rules: each mark has a conventional place, meaning, and length. These hardly ever coincide with the rhythms and pauses of the speaking subject and therefore end up by confining speech within grammatical and logical rules which it does not necessarily follow.[12]

All that can be hoped for is that in seeking to make the written word readable, that what Maura Cronin describes as the 'spontaneity' and 'freshness' of the oral interview was also retained.[13] However, this study is not exclusively based on oral testimonies. Documentary evidence forms a major part of the overall research, as do photographs and secondary written sources, in what is essentially a multi-disciplinary approach. The challenge has been to use the personal testimonies as a window to illuminate the issues raised by the decline and closure of the Dublin Cattle Market and what it tells us of the Irish livestock industry and Irish farming in the 1960s and early 1970s.

1. The mechanics of the Market

The Dublin Cattle Market was still Ireland's premier fat-stock sale when its last full decade in operation dawned. In fact, it was deemed so important to the livestock trade that the annual report from the Department of Agriculture carried averages from the market's sales.[1] The 'swinging sixties' shook Britain out of its post-war inertia but in Ireland change was a slower process and it took 13 years for developments in the livestock sector to finally undermine the Dublin market's commercial viability. Indeed, in 1957 the number of fat cattle sold in the market peaked at 249,776, while a record number of sheep was sold in 1960 when the figure topped 425,000.[2] The Dublin market was arguably among the leading livestock sales operations in Europe at the start of the 1960s and this was reflected in the mix of local and international buyers who visited each week to purchase stock. 'I remember my father and uncle saying that you could sell anything in the Dublin market, you could sell a goat if you wanted to,' recalled former sales-master Joe Barry.[3] This view is shared by many who sold and bought stock at the facility. In fact, Longford cattle dealer Jack Donlon could even put a name on one of the primary buyers of goats in the market. He claimed the purchaser was a man called Scally, who bought cheap livestock for Dublin Zoo.[4] However, these recollections related to novelty sales; the main business of the market in the period from 1960 to 1973 was, as it had always been, the sale of cattle and sheep. But how did the market work and why was it so influential in the livestock trade in Ireland generally? This chapter will outline the mechanics of the market and its importance.

As already stated, the Dublin Cattle Market was situated between Phibsboro and the quays, in an area bordered by Prussia Street, Aughrim Street and St Joseph's Road. The facilities were commissioned and built by Dublin Corporation and opened in 1863, with the market replacing a weekly cattle sale in the city, which was held in the nearby Smithfield area.[5] The Dublin Cattle Market, which was licensed and regulated by Dublin Corporation, was for many decades the final sales point for thousands of cattle that were bought each week at fairs or off farms around the country. A high proportion of these cattle were transported to holdings in Meath, Kildare and Dublin to be fattened and finished, although some were sold directly in the market. Joe Barry explained that livestock going directly for sale were kept initially in cattle parks around Dublin for two or three days to rest and settle the animals. These parks were located in what are now city suburbs such as Cabra, Finglas and Castleknock. 'I remember our park was about thirty acres and it wasn't far from Cabra

2. Sale day at the Dublin Cattle Market in the 1950s.

convent … I remember my father saying it was the best land he ever owned,' Joe recalled.[6] The cattle and sheep were then moved into lairages or yards beside the market, before being finally brought to the sales pens in the market on the morning of the sale. After the livestock were sold, they were driven along the streets to the nearby abattoirs, or down the Liffey quays to the docks at North Wall to be exported to Britain or the Continent. The size of the cattle market and the manner in which it was laid out is clearly illustrated in figure 2. The livestock were held in a series of pens. The cattle were tied and tethered to a rail at one end of these open enclosures, with their back ends facing out into alleyways that ran between the rows of pens. These alleyways allowed buyers to move easily between the various pens of cattle, as is obvious from figure 2. The photograph also captures the size of the market, while the tenements in the background illustrate its location in the heart of the city. Within six years of opening in 1863 the cattle market had penning for 3,020 cattle and 10,200 sheep. However, the market continued to expand and by the 1950s it had penning for over 5,000 cattle.[7] The sheds that can be seen dotted around the market in figure 2 acted as offices for the various sales-masters. Joe Barry recalled preparing sales dockets for butchers in these offices and getting 'hell absolutely' if the paperwork wasn't ready in time because the butcher wouldn't pay until the following week.[8] The story illustrates the pressure that was on both sellers and buyers to get transactions completed as quickly as possible. Boats and butcher shops awaited and the purchasers had to have their business finalized before most people started their working day. Like meat markets such as Rungis in Paris and Smithfield in London, the Dublin Cattle Market started early, with the gates opening for livestock at 3 a.m. and the sale starting at 5 a.m. The working day was over by 12 noon at the latest.

Livestock drovers were responsible for moving the cattle and sheep within the market, and later to the abattoirs and the docks. Invariably Dubliners, the drovers were instantly recognizable by their long yellow cloth coats and the skill of these men in handling cattle was accepted by all who worked in the market.[9] Joe Barry's regard for the drovers is obvious from the manner in which he talked of Sam and Christy McKeever, the father and son from Cabra who worked on their stand.

> The McKeevers were wonderful men, there was Sam and Christy – Sam was the father, Christy was the son and they were big powerful men. They had hands like shovels and they were serious characters in terms of being able to physically handle cattle. And when you think about it, a big bullock that has never been tied up before and they ... had to be tied with ropes along the railing. And this all had to be done in the early morning before the main business got going and they did it with extraordinary speed. But I suppose their size and their bulk helped, plus their sheer skill at lassoing cattle and dragging them in by the rope and just getting them in a line against the railing.[10]

Meath farmer Joe Ward was similarly impressed by the skill of the drovers. His memoir refers to the 'pen men' who worked in the Dublin market and whom he described as 'absolute experts' at their job. He recalled the skill and speed they displayed when tethering the cattle for the sale.

> The pen man would look them [the cattle] over quickly and would put them in order, the tallest beast at the top, and then the next tallest, down to the smallest one at the end. While two men held the cattle up to the pen, a third man put a rope around its neck and tied it around the bar. It took him thirty seconds or less. The rope was pulled in such a way that if the beast pulled, it had not hurt its neck in any way; the pull was on the iron bar of the pen.[11]

Ward's appreciation of the skill and technique displayed by the market's drovers echoes the observation of Michael Schwalbe who notes that people may carve out what he describes as 'microspheres of craft' in ordinary and seemingly mundane tasks. He maintained that workers can 'invent, solve problems and learn new things even if no one notices.'[12] However, in the Dublin market the work of the drovers was generally, though not always, noticed and valued. Former drover Bobby Walsh bemoaned the lack of respect that was shown to him and former colleagues in the market – 'being a drover had a very bad name, people always looked down on them'.[13] However, this was not the experience of Meath farmer and sales-master Jimmy Cosgrave. He described the drovers as 'lovely fellas' who were excellent men to work cattle. He recounted how different lots of cattle could get mixed together when they were taken to the scales to be weighed:

> there could be four lots of cattle in the line and there could be 20 cattle in it and out of the 20 cattle there could be 10 different owners and sellers and there could be maybe five different buyers ... and they'd sort them out.

He also recalled the drovers on bicycles driving lines of cattle 'half a mile' long down through the heart of Dublin to the boats at the North Wall and maintained that there was rarely a problem.

> The drover would let them out and they'd just run along, I mean, the cattle would be two or three abreast, with their heads down and they going on along and there'd be lads at all the crosses but once they got going straight they'd go straight.[14]

Some of the drovers used dogs to help them move the cattle and sheep. Bobby Walsh explained that most of these were collies crossed with terriers, or 'short hairs' as he called them. And some had rings in their noses, like a pig ring, to stop them biting the sheep.[15] Jack Donlon recalled seeing the dogs at work in the market and maintained that they were 'powerful dogs'.[16] Working the sheep and cattle in and out between the traffic and trams was all part of the job, as Bobby Walsh pointed out:

> At the time there were trams and we'd be going down with the cattle and sheep and the tram would come behind you and there was a bell that'd go 'ding, ding, ding' and you had to try and get the cattle and sheep apart to let him pass. And in a few minutes more a tram would be coming the other way. So the old dogs, when the tram would be coming, we'd send them over and they'd bark. Ah, there were some good dogs in Dublin.[17]

Bobby Walsh also recalled travelling to the cattle parks to feed cattle or to bring them into the cattle market.

> In the summer we'd have to go out in the fields because the animals would be on the land, not in the yard. Cattle lands was all around Ashtown, Blanchardstown, Finglas, Castleknock ... three or seven or eight miles back. And you'd get a wet shirt sweating, feeding the cattle with pulp and

turnips and getting oats and barley and hay and carrying buckets to feed them. And we used to lay in the hay. Now wet weather in the wintertime was the worst but you'd always be warm because it was a galloping game.[18]

Butchers, meat factories and livestock exporters were the main buyers of the cattle herded by the drovers. The butchers serviced the capital's fresh meat trade, the factories supplied sides of beef and lamb to the growing wholesale butcher market, as well carcass beef and lamb for export markets, while the livestock exporters bought and shipped cattle and sheep live. The exported cattle were mainly bound for England and Scotland, but significant numbers of cattle were also shipped to Germany and Holland. As already stated, the market originally sold mainly finished or fat cattle. These are animals that are ready for slaughter. Sales of store cattle – younger stock that are 18 months to two years old and still six months to a year away from being finished – were also held but this trade was carried out on the margins of the market by auctioneering firms such as Ganlys, Gavin Lows and Craigies.[19] However, the 'prime buyers' were the exporters, as Joe Barry recalled:

> When you started off in the morning you were obviously on the watch for the good guys, the men with the money, the men who wanted good stock ... There was Palm, he was one of them, Buitelaar was another ... [and] a number of Englishmen whose names escape me.[20]

The two buyers mentioned, Heinrick Palm and Frans Buitelaar, were German and Belgian nationals respectively. Both Palm and Buitelaar were significant shippers of cattle from Ireland to the Continent from the 1950s until the 1970s. Palm, who lived at Lunestown House, a 500-acre estate near Mullingar, also shipped cattle from South America to Europe in the 1950s and 1960s, and was a signifcant buyer of Irish beef for the German market.[21] However, cattle importers from Britain still dominated the Dublin market in the 1960s, as they had done since its opening a century earlier. Live exports of cattle and sheep had always been vital to the farming sector but had been damaged by the Economic War of the 1930s and the Second World War. The number of cattle shipped live increased steadily in the late 1940s and the trade was worth £22.7 million in value terms by 1950.[22] This represented almost one-third of the country's total exports. Between 1950 and 1960 the number of cattle exported 'on the hoof' varied from year to year but generally averaged around 500,000 head.[23] As Liam Clare pointed out, English buyers and the increasingly influential meat factory sector took the bulk of the heavy bullocks on offer.[24] The cattle for export to Britain were shipped the evening of the sale. Since the English buyers were weekly visitors to the market, they were well known and would usually deal with particular sales-masters. The itinerary for their trips to Dublin rarely changed, Liam Clare explained:

English buyers would arrive the evening before the market via the mail-boat and lodge overnight in the City Arms Hotel or in local bed and breakfast accommodation. Alternatively, they might come in on a 'dawn flight', assemble their lots of three hundred or four hundred cattle, go off for breakfast, settle their account, hand over their purchases to a shipping agent and fly out again.[25]

The English buyers were widely respected as excellent judges of cattle. Jimmy Cosgrave remembers the English buyers being very particular about the stock they bought. He recalled that they were always looking for 'a particular type of beast' and, therefore, they might only buy one animal that suited their specifications from a pen of ten.[26] This observation suggests that the English meat market was more discerning and demanding than its Irish equivalent and that the buyers visiting Dublin were seeking quality as well as quantity. Meanwhile, the presence in the Dublin market of Continental buyers, such as the aforementioned Palm and Buitelaar, demonstrated the unique position Ireland enjoyed in the 1950s of having surplus supplies of live cattle and carcass beef, and the extensive trading links that were established as a consequence. Indeed, Raymond Keogh states that contacts in the Low Countries had been established in the late 1940s when buyers from Holland and Belgium bought significant numbers of Irish cattle for fattening and slaughter. They were forced to import Irish cattle as livestock numbers in both countries had not recovered from the losses suffered during the Second World War.[27]

If the exporters and factories were the main buyers of bullocks, then the butchers dominated the trade for fat heifers. Gerard O'Kelly was one of the many butchers who bought stock in the Dublin Cattle Market. The family had a butcher's shop in Dolphin's Barn in Dublin, and he recalled going to the market every Wednesday morning with his father to buy two heifers and six sheep for their shop. These were bought live and slaughtered the same day in the Dublin City Abattoir, which was located across from the market on the North Circular Road. The meat was delivered by the abattoir, which was run by Dublin Corporation, the day after the cattle were killed. Although not from a farming background, the O'Kellys learned how to buy stock in the market by experience, Gerard explained.[28] Since the cattle and sheep were bought on the hoof, the O'Kellys had to estimate the carcass weight of the animals. Gerard admitted that this process was 'hit and miss' and they never knew whether the stock were cheap or dear until they were killed and the meat yield was calculated. However, the O'Kellys dealt with the same sales-master each week, Johnny Mulligan, and this provided a degree of informal insurance.[29]

These business relationships, which had a personal feel to them, were a recurring feature of the market and acted as a safety net for both the buyer and the seller. The sales-master was guaranteed to be paid if the same butcher was dealing with him on a regular basis, while the butcher had the opportunity for redress if he bought a particularly poor animal. The importance of protecting these relationships was also commented on by Jimmy Cosgrave. Where a butcher was charged too much for an animal he would be back the next week and 'he wouldn't be too long telling you,' Jimmy recalled. He said the redress usually involved doing a deal on the next animal he bought. The level of trust in the market was exemplified by the credit arrangements operated for the butchers. Many worked off weekly credit, Jimmy said, with cattle that were bought one week being paid for the next. However, he insisted they 'never had a bother with payment'.[30] These personal relationships also facilitated greater specialization in the market, with sales-masters supplying specific types of animals for particular buyers. Indeed, purchases by individual butchers in the Dublin Cattle Market reflected the social divisions within the city since it was possible to gauge the prosperity of a shop's clientele, and thereby a particular area, by the quality of livestock he bought. Joe Barry confirmed this when he explained that the 'butchers all had different needs'. Shops with a 'high class trade' took prime cattle of the 'highest conformation'. In contrast, butchers in the poorer districts bought old cows that were close to 'their sell-by date' because their customers wanted cheaper beef cuts.[31]

Whatever about reflecting class differences in the capital, the Dublin market had a much more tangible impact on the livestock trade nationally. The market's profile and the numbers of cattle and sheep traded each week meant it was still the premier livestock sale in the country in the early 1960s. Dublin remained the final point of sale for a high proportion of the country's finished and store cattle up until the mart movement took the lead in cattle and sheep sales in the mid 1960s. In the words of Liam Clare, the market tended to set 'the baseline for prices' nationally.[32] The market's standing among farmers was enhanced by the weekly reports carried on RTÉ and in the *Irish Farmers' Journal* and national newspapers.[33] These detailed the numbers of cattle sold, the tone of the trade, the main buyers and, most importantly, the prices paid. As Liam Clare points out, Michael Dillon was the best known agricultural correspondent in Ireland and his radio reports on the Dublin Market prices were listened to 'all over the country'.[34] This is confirmed by Limerick farmer Micheál O'Brien. He recalled how farmers in his area listened to the reports from the Dublin market before cattle were taken to fairs in Limerick or Rathkeale. Asked why this was done, he answered simply: 'Because you got the up-to-date value of your cattle.'[35] The fact that the sales-masters and dealers who were trading in the Dublin market bought their cattle at fairs around the country also guaranteed the market's influence in the trade nationally. Jimmy Cosgrave sourced cattle for the market from neighbours in Meath, but he also bought stock at fairs in the west. 'My people would have gone to fairs in Tuam and Athenry and Ballinasloe,' he says.[36] Similarly, Joe Barry tells of going to Wexford with his father to buy 'stall-fed' cattle for the market.[37] Since the prices paid to farmers by these sales-masters were based on returns available from the Dublin market, it is clear that the Prussia Street sale ultimately set, or at least heavily influenced, prices right across the country.

By the mid-1960s the Dublin Cattle Market's position as the premier outlet for Irish finished stock was being threatened by the development of the livestock marts' network and the growing importance of the meat-processing sector. Indeed, Central Statistics Office data shows that processed beef exports increased from 6,500 tonnes to 55,000 tonnes between 1950 and 1965.[38] The greater competition between the meat factories and exporters is highlighted in a report in the *Irish Independent* on 2 May 1970, which stated that English cattle buyers were struggling to compete with the Irish processors for cattle.[39] Meanwhile, between 1960 and 1970 the number of cattle marts increased from 72 to 177.[40] These trends obviously had a negative impact on the fortunes of the Dublin market. The number of cattle sold in the market each week fell sharply between 1965 and 1970. While 3,088 fat and store cattle were sold at the Prussia Street facility on the fourth Wednesday in April 1965, by 1970 this figure had fallen to 552.[41] The significant reduction in cattle numbers seriously undermined the financial viability of the market. The sales centre lost money each year from 1957, but the annual deficit increased during the second half of the 1960s as cattle numbers declined and reached £30,000 by 1970.[42] These losses were subvented by Dublin Corporation. With the Irish livestock sector changing radically, reform of the Dublin Cattle Market was required for the institution to survive.

2. Challenges and changes

The 1970s are remembered as a decade of unprecedented change in Irish farming. EEC membership in 1973 brought guaranteed markets but more importantly it brought guaranteed commodity prices and farm incomes rose sharply as a result. Improved returns were to drive investment in the sector as farmers strove to make the most of the opportunities that Europe's Common Agricultural Policy (CAP) presented. However, the foundations for many of the positive developments of the 1970s were laid in the preceding decade. One of the most fundamental shifts involved the manner in which livestock were sold. In the ten years from 1960 to 1970 the country's fairs were almost totally eclipsed by the newly formed livestock marts as the primary means for farmers to sell their stock. The period also saw greater specialization in farming, as mixed holdings began to be replaced by single-enterprise and dual-enterprise operations such as dairy and beef, or beef and sheep, or beef and tillage units. The establishment of Bord Bainne in 1961 for the marketing of dairy produce, and Córas Beostoic agus Feola (CBF) in 1969 to promote Irish meat and livestock exports illustrated the central role government continued to play in the farm sector.[1] Meanwhile, improvements in animal breeding, feeding and husbandry meant the scientific and technical elements of farming began to be accepted as critical promoters of profitability.[2] This was the rapidly evolving farming environment that the Dublin Cattle Market had to cope with in the 1960s. It was one that offered exciting opportunities but much more serious challenges for an institution that was already struggling to adapt to the changed trading landscape. The government's determination to support and promote the home-processing of beef, and the impact this had on exports of fat cattle, signalled a major revision of policy. Equally, the Department of Agriculture's Bovine TB eradication programme of 1957–65 caused difficulties for the live trade. However, it was the manner in which the Dublin market adapted to the threat posed by the growing power and popularity of the livestock marts that ultimately determined its future.

The development of the livestock mart network was a response to growing farmer dissatisfaction with the manner in which cattle were traditionally purchased at the country fairs and the prices they received for their stock.[3] By 1960 marts had been operating successfully in Britain for over eighty years and the emerging Irish farm organizations were anxious to emulate this success. However, price was not the only consideration that influenced the drive to establish marts. Competition for stock, the transparency of the sale process, and a guarantee of payment were all equally important factors. In the marts, the presence of both farmers and exporters ensured competition for stock, while the open bidding provided transparency. On the issue of payment, Maurice Colbert observed that it was 'one thing getting a price for your animal' but to ensure that you were paid for stock was 'just as important'.[4] The open nature of mart sales was in sharp contrast to the archaic traditions of the fair. The entire process of agreeing a sale at the fair was governed by defined conventions, as Raymond Keogh recalls. Cattle were sold in groups of varying weights and quality, with farmer sellers often attempting to disguise the presence of one or two poorer cattle in a batch of better stock. Keogh's recollection of buying cattle at a fair clearly illustrates the curious traditions involved.

> Protocol required the vendor to put his cattle on price. Only then was the buyer allowed to propose a lower offer. When that was rejected, as custom required, the intending buyer should turn away, visibly disappointed, departing slowly enough to permit easy recapture. At the heel of the hunt a deal would begin to materialize, facilitated by the unexplained but nigh-inevitable appearance of the tangler. He would seize both men's right hands, struggling theatrically to join them together as all the while bids, counter-bids, denials, accusations and counter-accusations filled the air. If, at length, a deal were struck, both buyer and seller must spit on his right hand before pressing the flesh to signify closure.[5]

The etiquette of the fairs was mirrored in the conventions of the Dublin Cattle Market. Joe Barry explains that once a buyer was involved in negotiations with a seller he could not be interrupted in 'any shape or form', nor could any other party express an interest in the cattle until the haggling process had irrevocably broken down.[6] Interestingly, similar customs and practices are noted by Victor C. Uchendu in his study on the principles of haggling in peasant markets from Haiti to West Africa.[7] The archaic traditions involved in selling cattle at fairs and markets, and the fact that many farmers believed dealers exerted too much control over proceedings, facilitated the rise of the livestock marts. Former *Irish Farmers' Journal* correspondent, John Shirley, described the fairs as a 'desperate way of selling cattle' where farmers were at the 'whim of the dealers'. Colbert tells of walking cattle to the fair in Dungarvan, Co. Waterford, in the 1950s and being met by dealers on the way into the town who attempted to buy the cattle cheaply prior to the sale by predicting a very depressed trade. Similarly, John Shirley recalls how the dealers invariably had a story of a boatload of beef from Argentina driving down prices in Britain.[8]

However, such stories were sometimes correct; a sharp cattle price drop in the Dublin market in March 1963 was blamed on heavy shipments of Argentine beef into Britain.[9] John Shirley and Raymond Keogh also point to the manner in which towns were 'mucked up' by the fairs and the cleaner environment that the marts brought.[10] The comments of both Colbert and Shirley also point to a historic resentment of livestock dealers among farmers, and suggests that the majority of livestock owners were glad to abandon the fairs and give their business to marts – many of which were owned and controlled by farmer co-operatives. This was particularly the case in the southern half of the country where the dairy co-operative structure was already strong. Indeed, 14 of the 27 co-operative mart societies operating in 1966 were located in Munster. Sales in these marts totalled almost £18 million or close to 80 per cent of the overall turnover in co-operative marts.[11] However, it would be incorrect and simplistic to portray the relationship between farmers and cattle traders generally as being characterized by hostility. The experiences of Joe Barry and Jimmy Cosgrave clearly illustrate the strong and long-lasting business links and friendships sales-masters and dealers had fostered with individual farmers over years and even generations. Indeed, Jimmy Cosgrave pointed out that his family bought cattle every year at the fairs 'in Tuam and Athenry and Ballinasloe', and they were well known by the farmers there.[12] Similarly, Joe Barry recounted travelling to Wexford to buy stock:

> We'd drive down and he'd [Joe Barry's father] go around buying stall-fed cattle, fat cattle that had been tied up in stalls, from farms dotted all around the Enniscorthy area. Those cattle would be sent by rail up to Dublin and they would then go in to the lairages. He would also buy fat cattle in the summer, obviously from farmers all around Ireland.[13]

Both these examples suggest that sales-masters were dealing with the same farmers year after year. These relationships could not have been sustained if the farmers were not benefitting from them. Clearly, the relationship between farmers and dealers was complex and multi-layered. Equally, Cronin cites the social intermingling between farmers and dealers that was a feature of most country fairs.[14] Even so, the late 1950s and early 1960s was certainly a period when the old ties that existed between cattle traders and farmers were strained. However, there was also an acceptance among some sales-masters that the marts were a fairer way of selling livestock. Commenting on the changeover from the fairs to marts, Raymond Keogh insisted that it was a 'logical' and 'natural' development, because the manner of doing business in the fairs and Dublin market had become 'antiquated'.[15]

The co-operative marts offered a mechanism to weaken the dealers' and exporters' influence on the cattle trade. This was recognized by the National Farmers' Association (NFA) and the Irish Creamery Milk Suppliers' Association (ICMSA), as well as by the co-operative umbrella body ICOS. From the outset the marts posed a serious threat not only to the dealers who controlled the supply of livestock to the Dublin Cattle Market, but also to the sales-masters who sold the cattle and sheep, and to the exporters who shipped the animals to

Britain and the Continent. Moreover, the marts posed an immediate threat to hundreds of fairs around the country where the dealers and exporters sourced their livestock supplies. The extent of the challenge posed by the farmer-owned businesses was confirmed when the fledgling marts targeted the British export trade directly. The 1956 annual report of the Irish Agricultural Organisations' Society (IAOS), which later became ICOS, records that representatives from the Kilkenny and Waterford mart societies, which were formed that same year, visited England 'for the purposes of opening up an export trade'. It adds that the contacts made had proven 'very valuable and the resulting export business has been very successful.'[16]

The dealers and sales-masters responded to the challenge posed by the marts by encouraging their members to stay away from the sales rings. In its 1956 annual report, and in meetings with the NFA, the IAOS claimed that the lack of support from 'professional buyers' amounted to a 'virtual boycott of the co-operative marts'.[17] This dispute between the marts and the cattle dealers and exporters persisted through the late 1950s and into the 1960s. Indeed, the dispute impacted the trade in the Dublin market, with the Irish National Livestock Traders' Union boycotting sales-masters who sold cattle that were purchased previously in regional marts. They also attempted to prevent the export of such animals.[18] Jack Donlon recalled a consignment of cattle being driven from the Dublin market and into the surrounding streets because they had been purchased through the marts in north Tipperary and Offaly. While the exact story cannot be independently verified, there is no reason to doubt that some incident involving the removal of stock from the market took place.[19] Indeed, it could be argued that the importance of this story is in the portrayal of the passions the dispute aroused among the various parties, rather than in the detail. As Portelli explains, there are no 'false' oral sources:

> The diversity of oral history consists in the fact that 'wrong' statements are still psychologically 'true' and that this truth may be equally as important as factually reliable accounts.[20]

Despite the early success of the marts, the livestock traders had not given up hope of the fairs surviving. A meeting of the Irish Cattle Traders' and Stockowners' Association in November 1962 'noted with satisfaction' that recent fairs in Tullamore, Edenderry, Tyrrellspass and Mullingar had been successful and it was agreed that a second fair in Mullingar would be advertised if livestock exporters agreed to offer support.[21] However, as early as September 1961 the dealers' campaign was under pressure and there were complaints at an association meeting that some livestock traders were using 'back-door methods' to attend marts. One delegate warned the meeting that there would be no fairs left if dealers simply 'surrendered'. However, not all agreed with this view and the meeting was told that it was difficult to expect dealers 'whose fairs were

3. Fr J. Coyne performing the official opening of Nenagh Mart, Co. Tipperary in 1957.

gone' to remain loyal to the boycott.[22] In the end, however, the weight of cattle numbers being sold through the marts meant the boycott had to be abandoned.

The pace of the transition from fairs to marts varied regionally as it took time to establish a network of sales rings. Each co-operative society had to raise around £15,000 in capital from farmers to fund the mart's development. A further £8,000 to £10,000, which was financed by bank loans, was used for set-up costs and working capital.[23] Private marts needed the backing of business interests to fund their development. Indeed, many of the early private marts were set up by auctioneering firms, such as the Warrens in Enniscorthy, the Pottertons in Trim and Delvin, and the Ganlys and Craigies in Ashbourne, Co. Meath. The IAOS annual report of 1955 acknowledged the difficulties facing the new enterprises and listed the provision of adequate capital and lack of experience in running livestock sales operations as the obvious pitfalls.[24]

However, the co-operative movement had successfully run the country's creameries for three generations and these societies provided the springboard for the move into livestock sales. In 1956 there were six co-operative societies formed and three marts operating, these were in Waterford, Kilkenny and Bunclody, Co. Wexford.[25] By the end of the 1960s there were thirty co-operative mart societies, many of them like Cork Marts and Clare Marts had multiple outlets.[26] In addition, the network of private operations had expanded steadily and included sixty-one centres by 1970.[27] The sudden growth in the number of marts had an obvious impact on the livestock trade. As the marts took over from the fairs, the numbers sold through the auction rings increased exponentially. This is reflected in the value of the sales they handled. In 1961 total livestock sales in the co-operative marts were valued at £7,638,328.[28] However, this figure had reached £46,073,587 by 1969.[29]

While the impact of the marts on the Dublin Cattle Market started slowly, it quickly gathered pace. An *Irish Farmers' Journal* headline from May 1964 that read 'Dublin Market in Danger' clearly indicates that there were already fears for its long-term viability.[30] The report highlighted the extent to which cattle sales through the market itself had fallen sharply between 1960 and 1963. In contrast, total sales in the private auction rings operated within the market by auctioneering firms Ganlys, Gavin Lows and Manor Sales experienced a significant increase. The *Irish Farmers' Journal* report stated that the number of cattle sold in the market itself fell from 170,000 in 1960 to 107,000 in 1963. During the same period the volume of cattle sales handled by the market's three auction rings went from 102,000 to 230,000.[31] These figures broadly tally with the official Dublin Corporation records. These show that the number of cattle and calves sold in the Dublin market stood at 207,759 in 1961–2, this figure fell to 138,437 in 1962–3 and hit 112,132 for 1963–4. In the same three-year period sales in the auction rings went from 149,197 to 237,828.[32] It could be argued that Dublin's continued importance as an export centre was confirmed by these figures since the total number of cattle sold in both the market and its auction rings had held at around 350,000 animals per year. However, the data also suggest that the main buyers of cattle in Dublin – the exporters, slaughter plants and butchers – were displaying a clear preference for auction sales. This was a worrying development for the market, given that farmers around the country were showing a similar predisposition. Those involved in the market at this time admit that they did not experience it in its prime but in its decline.[33] This view appears to be confirmed by the fact that the same number of cattle were sold through Dublin each year between 1960 and 1964, although the national herd increased from 4.74 million to 4.95 million in the same period.[34] In short, Dublin was steadily losing its share of total cattle sales. A more in-depth look at cattle export figures also illustrates the malaise that was taking hold. While it is difficult to establish accurately the proportion of the cattle sold through Dublin that subsequently went for export, it is estimated that the figure was in the region of 80–5 per cent, which equates to between 280,000 and 300,000 a year in the period from 1960 to 1964.[35] However, as can be seen from figure 4, this is well below the total number of cattle exported live from the state as a whole in both 1963 and 1964. Indeed, if the number of cattle sold for export in Dublin at the time is taken to be 300,000, this represents just thirty-eight per cent of Ireland's total live cattle exports in 1964 which stood at 793,770.[36] There was nothing new in the export of cattle from regional centres and both Jack Donlon and Micheál O'Brien recall stock being bought in Longford and Limerick in the 1950s for export through Dublin Port and Waterford respectively.[37]

Beef Industry Statistics			
Year	Herd size	Live cattle exports	Beef exports (Tonnes)
1955	4.483 million	618,000	17,000
1960	4.741 million	542,000	48,000
1961	4.713 million	722,400	74,700
1962	4.742 million	575,250	59,800
1963	4.880 million	662,760	61,700
1964	4.952 million	793,770	52,700
1965	5.359 million	596,590	55,000
1966	5.590 million	624,950	70,000
1967	5.588 million	670,980	148,000
1968	5.572 million	625,420	117,000
1969	5.688 million	552,000	122,000
1970	5.956 million	529,180	140,400
1973	7.113 million	430,000	131,100
1975	7.168 million	695,310	270,000

4. Live cattle and beef exports from Ireland, 1955–75. Figures based on CSO and Department of Agriculture data.

To put it simply, the Dublin market did not have a monopoly on the trade. In fact, it is clear that both British buyers and Irish exporters did an increasing proportion of their business directly with the marts during the second half of the 1960s as the farmer-owned livestock sales centres took a firmer grip on cattle trade. Jimmy Cosgrave recounts how one Limerick-based dealer collected British buyers at Dublin Airport, drove them to marts in the west and arranged transport to England for the cattle they bought. He then returned the UK traders to the capital for their flight home. The Limerick cattle agent was paid an agreed commission on each animal purchased.[38] Similarly, Cork Marts developed direct contacts with buyers in England for supplies of Irish cattle.[39] The simplicity of such arrangements increasingly undermined the role of the Dublin market as the 1960s progressed.

The TB eradication scheme introduced by the Department of Agriculture in 1957 also caused serious disruption for the Dublin market.[40] The eradication scheme was established after the British authorities informed their Irish counterparts that future cattle imports into the UK could be limited to animals that were tested and clear of TB by 1961.[41] This problem had the potential to cripple live exports and the Irish government successfully sought to delay the introduction of the restrictions while pouring resources into combating the disease. In fact, by 1961–2 spending on the TB eradication scheme exceeded £9 million or one-quarter of the overall agriculture budget.[42] The immediate impact on the Dublin market was that special sales had to be arranged every Tuesday for stock that had been tested just once for TB. Since two clear tests were, in fact, required to establish that an animal was free of TB, the cattle sold at these sales were not deemed completely clear.[43] These 'once-tested' animals were allowed to be exported to the UK by the British authorities as an interim measure, although they were subject to movement restrictions. However, the incidence of TB within the Irish cattle herd dropped dramatically as the eradication programme gathered pace and by 1963 all cattle sold through the Dublin market were fully tested for the disease. Indeed, by January 1963 all cattle exported from Ireland to England had to be TB-free.[44] Unfortunately, that was not the end of the disruption. Proof that a particular animal had been tested and was TB-free necessitated the introduction of individual cards for each animal. This card carried the same number as a tag on the beast's ear. Ensuring that all the animals' tags and cards matched meant a lot more work for the farmers, dealers, sales-masters and exporters, and was extremely unpopular as a consequence. It also resulted in a serious problem of tag and card swapping, as the value of an untested animal could be significantly increased by giving it a 'TB-free' identity.[45]

A shift in government policy to promote and support the beef-processing industry more actively added to the pressures on the Dublin Cattle Market. This changed approach was illustrated in the provisions of the Anglo-Irish Free Trade Agreement (AIFTA) of December 1965. Under the agreement Ireland undertook to maintain exports of store cattle to Britain at 638,000 head each year. In addition, the British agreed to extend UK subsidy payments under the Fatstock Guarantee Scheme to imports of 25,000 tons of Irish processed beef and 5,500 tons of Irish processed lamb. These subsidies had traditionally been limited to store cattle exports to the UK.[46] The 1966 decision by the Minister of Agriculture, Charles Haughey, to guarantee Irish exchequer supports on all prime beef exports to the UK – at the same rate as the British AIFTA payments – was a further contributor to the dramatic growth in carcass beef production.[47] Haughey's decision meant the Irish state effectively established an open-ended support mechanism for beef exports to Britain in excess of the 25,000 tons covered by the AIFTA.[48] The decision was consistent with Haughey's vision of developing a vibrant food industry in Ireland.[49] As Longford-based meat processors John Lyons recalled, 'Haughey was keen to get away from live shipping, and get the meat industry going'.[50] Like the AIFTA beef supports, only top quality heifers and bullocks were eligible for payments under Haughey's Carcass Beef Export Guarantee Scheme.[51] The AIFTA and Haughey's initiative had an immediate impact on the Irish livestock trade. Store cattle exports to Britain increased from 396,400 head in 1966 to 591,500 in 1968.

However, fat cattle sales collapsed, falling from 205,000 to 16,000 head in the same period.[52] This was due to increased competition from Irish meat factories for finished cattle, and the requirement that live animals had to be retained for two months on UK farms to qualify for the fatstock guarantee payment. Since fat cattle were ready to kill at the time they were sold in the Dublin market, British buyers were not willing to hold them for an additional two months to secure the fatstock guarantee payment. In contrast, Irish factories qualified for the support payment if the cattle were slaughtered and exported to Britain as beef. As Liam Clare notes, the changes meant that between 1965 and 1970, the trade for fat cattle in Dublin, which was considered the mainstay of the market, 'virtually disappeared'.[53]

Earlier in the decade the ratio between the export of fat cattle and unfinished younger store animals was relatively even, although it fluctuated according to price. The number of fat cattle exported in 1960–1 was just under 230,000, while the number of store cattle shipped was almost 340,000. These levels compared to exports of 360,000 store cattle in 1959–60 and just 80,000 fat cattle.[54] Since exports dominated the cattle trade and Britain was by far the most important outlet, prices in the Dublin market, and in Ireland generally, were effectively set by the English and Scottish buyers. However, trade agreements between the two countries ensured that Ireland remained the primary source of live cattle imports for Britain. Ireland's dominance of the trade was helped by what Daly has described as a '*de facto* monopoly' because continental cattle were excluded from Britain on health grounds. Indeed, it is estimated that between a quarter and one-third of 1.5 million head finished each year by UK farmers in the 1950s and early 1960s were born on Irish farms.[55] Irish cattle also had the advantage of qualifying for the aforementioned UK subsidies paid under the British Fatstock Guarantee Scheme once they were kept by British buyers for a minimum of two months. These subsidies were known as deficiency payments. This support scheme effectively set a base price for stock in Britain and enabled traders to make a healthy profit on imported cattle thanks to the substantial differential that existed between British and Irish prices. The Department of Agriculture's annual report for 1960–1 put the standard price for British stock at 167s. per hundred-weight (cwt), while the average price paid in March 1961 at the Dublin market was 139s. 9d. per hundred-weight.[56] Given that ten hundred-weight was generally the weight of finished cattle at the time, this meant Irish fat animals were making close to £70 per head on average in 1961, with their British counterparts worth £83–4 per head. This left a margin of around £13 per animal for the English and Scottish buyers. However, the AIFTA deal of 1965 changed the dynamics of the livestock trade.

The extension of the fatstock guarantee payment to carcass beef was a serious blow to the Dublin Cattle Market as it effectively ended the export trade for fat cattle to Britain which was a critical element of its business. John Shirley described the move as a 'sop' to the processing sector on the part of Charles

Haughey.[57] The decision was deeply resented by the Irish Cattle Traders' and Stockowners' Association, which represented many of the market's sales-masters. However, Haughey defended the change in policy. He informed the traders' association in February 1965 that shipments of live cattle had been so strong the previous year that the factories were unable to compete with the live exporters and that some government support for the processors was necessary.[58] Indeed, there was a 25 per cent reduction in the number of cattle killed by the slaughter plants in 1964, with throughput falling from 400,000 head to 300,000 animals as a result of stronger demand for fat cattle in Britain and the Continent.[59] Moreover, Haughey's determination to secure increased supports for the beef factories must be viewed in the context of the national economic expansion programmes that aimed to totally restructure the Irish economy in the 1960s. It was envisaged that the agriculture industry could become a major creator of wealth and rural employment by encouraging the dairy co-operatives and the meat factories to develop into food processors rather than continue as suppliers of bulk commodities. Ultimately, as Joe Lee points out, the government was disappointed in the capacity of faming to generate additional employment and help stem the flow of mass emigration. However, the extension of the fatstock guarantee to carcass beef was a game changer for meat processors and significantly helped in the expansion of the industry. This was also reflected in increased employment, with the numbers working directly in the sector growing from around 2,000 to 4,000 between 1960 and 1972.[60] As the figures in figure 4 show, the volume of beef exports almost trebled between 1965 and 1967, rising from 55,000 tons to 148,000 tons following the decision to extend the payment of fatstock guarantees to beef exports.[61] More specifically, Irish beef exports to Britain increased four-fold to almost 110,000 tons between 1965 and 1967, and averaged close to 100,000 tons up to 1971 – or almost 70 per cent of total foreign sales.[62] With the government continuing to provide support payments on beef exports, the slaughtering of cattle eclipsed the live export of animals for the first time in 1967 when 750,000 animals were killed and processed by local beef factories, compared to 645,000 cattle that were shipped on the hoof. The Store Cattle Study Group Report of 1968 attributed this profound shift in the Irish livestock industry to a 'massive injection of public money into the carcass beef trade'.[63] Indeed, close to £10 million in UK and Irish exchequer supports were paid to Irish beef processors between 1966 and 1970.[64] These subsidies were crucial to the development of the Irish meat processing industry; and to the significant growth in beef exports, which increased from 17,000 tonnes in 1955 to 270,000 tonnes by 1975.[65] The expansion in beef output recorded during this period was undoubtedly helped by Ireland's joining the EEC in 1973, and the development of schemes such as beef intervention which were funded by the Common Agricultural Policy (CAP). Even so, the changes in the structure of the Irish beef industry recorded during this period as a whole were pronounced and long-lasting.

The extension of fatstock guarantee payments to carcass beef was crucial to the development of the Irish beef industry, but it contributed to the demise of the Dublin Cattle Market. It gave the factories a significant competitive advantage over fat cattle exporters when it came to buying stock, and thereby undermined the trade for these animals in the market. In 1968 the value of the fatstock guarantee varied from £3 0s 9d. to £10 0s 3d. on finished animals that were making £90 to £100 a head.[66] Meanwhile, the Store Cattle Study Group Report estimated that the fatstock guarantee gave factory buyers a £15 per head advantage when competing with butchers or exporters for cattle in 1967.[67] The fatstock guarantee continued to distort trade in the Dublin market over its final years. The payment was still a source of irritation in 1970 for English exporters who were struggling to compete for cattle against buyers working for locally based beef factories. Indeed, a former manager at the International Meat Company's slaughter plant in Dublin's Grand Canal Street recalls the company's main buyer, Tom Hannigan, purchasing over 400 fat animals at the Dublin Cattle Market, and walking the livestock across the city to the plant.[68] However, as figure 4 confirms, the increased exports of processed beef were not delivered at the expense of reduced live exports. Indeed, live exports in 1975 exceeded 690,000 head – levels which had not been matched since the early 1960s – albeit that the vast majority of the livestock exported between 1965 and 1975 were store animals rather than fat cattle. However, as stated earlier, exports of beef reached 270,000 tonnes the same year. How was this possible? The answer lies in the growth of the national herd, which increased from 4.48 million cattle in 1955 to 7.16 million head twenty years later. The surge in dead meat exports was facilitated by this considerable expansion in cattle numbers.

The death of the fairs, the rise of the marts, the TB eradication scheme, and the growth of the meat processing sector combined to totally alter the structure of the Irish livestock industry. However, these changes also undermined the viability of the Dublin Cattle Market. This is evident from the declining numbers of cattle sold through the Prussia Street facility. While up to 4,000 cattle were sold in the market each week in the late 1950s, by Wednesday, 9 May 1973 just 325 animals were on offer. It was the last sale held in the Dublin Cattle Market.[69]

3. No market response

The steady decline in the Dublin Cattle Market's fortunes during the 1960s was a cause of grave concern for Dublin Corporation. As early as 1964 a review of the market's operations in Prussia Street was being sought by councillors, while the suitability of the inner city site for cattle sales and the mounting losses at both the market and the nearby Dublin City Abattoir were raised at corporation meetings.[1] The uncertainty around the future of the market undermined sales-masters' confidence, as is clear from the mixed messages coming from their representative bodies. At the same time as the Irish Cattle Traders' and Stockowners' Association was seeking to enforce a boycott of the marts, the Dublin Cattle Sales-masters' Association was calling on the corporation to provide auction sales facilities for fat cattle within the Dublin Cattle Market itself.[2] But was there anything the corporation or sales-masters could have done to arrest the market's decline? Or was there some way of reinvigorating the market and restoring its status as the premier Irish sales centre for fat cattle? This chapter will discuss why the Dublin Cattle Market was unable to react to the threat posed by the marts and factories; the ineffectual response of both the Dublin Corporation and sales-masters to changes in the livestock business; and how regulations and restrictions hindered trade at the Prussia Street site.

The worsening trading environment at the market is highlighted by the increasing losses which Dublin Corporation was forced to underwrite from the early 1960s. In 1962–3 total losses at the market amounted to £11,250 but the deficit for 1964–5 was £14,869.[3] However, the steady fall in the number of cattle sold through the market meant that by 1970 losses reached £22,000 and peaked at £39,000 two years later. By this time the local authority had opted to close the facility and was in the throes of a legal battle with the sales-masters as a result of this decision.[4] The losses were not confined solely to the sales complex. The Dublin City Abattoir, which, as noted previously, was located just across the North Circular Road from the market, was also losing money heavily. By 1968 annual losses in the Corporation-run slaughter facility exceeded £46,000.[5] However, the problems at the market had been flagged and were recognized a number of years earlier. The *Irish Farmers' Journal* headline from 1964 (cited in the previous chapter) which questioned the long-term viability of the Prussia Street operation was indicative of a view that the market was already in serious decline.[6] Indeed, the sense that the market's best days were well past by the early-1960s is also a recurring theme from the oral evidence. Both Joe Barry and Jimmy Cosgrave emphasize in their interviews that they experienced the market in decline rather than in its pomp.[7] Jimmy Cosgrave recalled how the market could not match the auction rings and mart sales for efficiency and convenience. He recounted how English traders could buy 'five or six hundred cattle' in less than 'three-quarters of an hour' in the auction rings run in the market grounds by Ganlys and Craigies. The clear implication is that this would not have been possible in the market itself.[8] Yet, sheep numbers in the market had just peaked in 1960 at 425,097, while Irish cattle exports were still running at over 662,000 in 1963.[9] Indeed, it is not unthinkable that the Dublin Cattle Market could have weathered the storm and maintained a profitable presence in the livestock sales business.

So why did the market not react to the changes in the sector? There is no simple answer to this question. The tightly regulated trading environment prevalent in the 1960s, however, particularly in the area of transport, certainly limited its ability to respond to the new realities. Strict regulations which confined the transport of livestock to CIÉ and other licensed hauliers were a serious impediment to the cattle trade in the 1960s.[10] The situation was exacerbated by a shortage of licences and the rigid enforcement of the regulations by the Gardaí, as Jimmy Cosgrave explained:

> You couldn't haul the cattle without a licence, and you couldn't get a licence, there were no licences to be got. There was only so many, they were like gold dust, something like the way the pubs are now.[11]

Cosgrave's family had a truck but not a haulage licence and legally they could only move cattle for themselves as a consequence. The difficulty in securing licences meant the haulage industry was viewed as lacking competition and capacity, with CIÉ considered inefficient and costly. Indeed, John McKeown of the Irish Livestock Exporters' and Traders' Association claimed that CIÉ were 25 to 30 per cent dearer than private hauliers, who he said gave a much better service.[12] This was certainly Jimmy Cosgrave's belief, who recalled CIÉ being 'fierce expensive' and 'uncompetitive'. He explained that neighbours who were selling cattle on Cosgrave's stand in the Dublin market had to walk the stock to their farm outside Enfield, Co. Meath, so they could be loaded and transported to Dublin. In this way the Cosgraves attempted to pass the cattle off as their own if stopped at Garda checkpoints on the road. Garda checks on trucks carrying livestock – to ensure the haulier had a valid licence or was not moving stock illegally – were not unusual at the time. 'The [Garda] Traffic Corp or the Haulage Corp and CIÉ would be mad looking to stop lads,' Jimmy Cosgrave claimed.[13] Individuals found transporting stock for others without a valid licence could face a sizeable fine, as court reports from the time confirm. Dublin cattle buyer William A. Smith was fined £20 and ordered to pay £14 2s. 4d. expenses at Clonmel Court in March 1966 for the illegal haulage of 28 cattle. In his defence Mr Smith claimed he 'was only doing what hundreds of other cattle agents were doing' and that it was a practice 'upon which the whole cattle trade and the future of the industry depended'.[14]

Men moving stock with tractors and cattle trailers were also liable to be checked and prosecuted if they were in breach of the statutes. A case in Roscrea Court in 1962 involving a local farmer who was prosecuted for transporting nine TB reactor cows to the local slaughter factory for a neighbour illustrates how strictly the regulations were enforced.[15] Jack Donlon recounted how country Gardaí, in plain clothes, were sent into the Dublin Cattle Market to identify people who were moving cattle illegally. However, everybody knew the Gardaí by their trousers, even the drovers' dogs. 'You'd hear a whistle at the far end of the market and you'd see the dogs sitting up … and the whole market knew that they [the Gardaí] were in.'[16] The strict transport regulations were a significant disruption to trade generally. Indeed, NFA president, T.J. Maher, claimed in January 1968 that small truck owners at marts were being 'badgered by the Gaurds'.[17] The transport regulations were particularly disruptive for the Prussia Street sales given the higher costs involved in moving cattle to Dublin rather than to local marts. Jack Donlon recalled how it cost £10 to transport a load of 12 finished cattle to the Dublin market from Longford in the late 1960s.[18] This equates to 16s. per head, a sizeable sum given that the dealers had to buy the cattle off the land, or at a fair or mart, and then sell them on quickly – and the transport cost came out of their margin. As a consequence, Jack Donlon only travelled to the Dublin market when he had a full load of cattle to sell.[19] When exporters began buying in marts around the country, it was obviously an option for farmers and dealers to go to the local sale with a smaller number of livestock rather than to Dublin. As Joe Barry pointed out:

> If you lived … around Athlone you weren't going to send your fat cattle up to the Dublin Cattle Market to sell, they would be sold locally and then railed on direct to the shippers.[20]

The transport regulations and costs were not a problem for the Dublin Cattle Market exclusively. Indeed, complaints were voiced at a meeting of the Irish Cattle Traders' and Stockowners' Association in January 1965 that CIÉ was 'not catering for the traffic from the fairs and marts throughout the country'.[21] However, the restrictions resulted in smaller entries in Dublin, mainly because the restrictions gave farmers and dealers another reason to trade locally. In addition, the issue illustrates the manner in which national policy – in this case the State's support for CIÉ's transport operations – impacted on the wider economy. In this instance, it impaired, albeit inadvertently, the Dublin market's ability to compete with the marts.

However, Liam Clare contends that weak governance on the part of Dublin Corporation was an even more significant factor in the market's failure to respond in a meaningful manner to the changed trading environment:

the city council [was] composed of forty-five individuals, virtually all non-specialists in the issues of the cattle trade, each of them with his or her own agenda, and each of them subject to pressures from a wide range of opposing vested interests. To have successfully adapted to the rapid reorganization of cattle marketing in the sixties, would appear to have been organizationally impossible.[22]

However, as Clare correctly points out, while the governance structures in the corporation contributed to the market's decline, there were other issues that restricted the freedom of the local authority to act and therefore undermined its ability to react to the profound changes taking hold.[23] The perceived legal obligation on Dublin Corporation to provide facilities for a livestock market in the city was one constraint, as was political interference in the affairs of the market, primarily from the Minister for Local Government but also from the Minister for Agriculture on occasion.[24] The manner in which legal considerations limited Dublin Corporation's room for manoeuvre was clearly illustrated when the Dublin Cattle Sales-masters' Association made the aforementioned call in October 1963 for auction rings to be built in the market for fat cattle sales.[25] This was one of the few initiatives that sought to counteract the growing influence of the marts. The plan appeared to be gaining momentum when in September 1964 the corporation's influential finance committee effectively endorsed it and recommended the construction of two auction rings in the market, even though such a move would legally trigger the closure of the existing sales rings, including those run by Ganlys and Craigies, since the derogation allowing them to operate was only valid as long as the council itself provided no auction facilities. The threat to the market's existing sales rings, which handled over 25 per cent of Ireland's store cattle exports to Britain, prompted an outcry from the auctioneering firms involved, as well as other vested interests such as the NFA and the Marine Port and General Workers' Union.[26] The Minister for Agriculture, Paddy Smith, also objected to the corporation's plans and he warned that legislation could be introduced to protect the existing auction rings if the local authority's proposals threatened their business.[27] In the wake of these interventions the initiative faltered.

Legal wrangles were also a factor in the failure of another proposal from the corporation in early 1966. In March that year the *Irish Farmers' Journal* reported that the corporation made an offer to the sales-masters to sell or lease them all or a section of the market, and that the sales-masters could then erect auction rings at their own expense.[28] However, this proposal also fell foul of the lawyers, as it was not clear whether in fact the local authority could be 'compelled to put up an auction ring for the accommodation of all other users of the market'.[29] This would obviously have brought additional costs on the local authority. However, there were also political considerations as the success of the plan hinged on the Minister for Local Government, Kevin Boland, agreeing to an increase in the tolls levied on cattle sales in the market. The corporation had fixed new rates in January 1966 but these were subject to ministerial sanction.[30] When the green light for the increased tolls was eventually given in November 1967, Minister Boland also sought a full review of the market's organization and control. This effectively forced the corporation and the sales-masters to make decisions on the long-term future of the sales complex and Liam Clare is correct in his assessment that it allowed the local authority to pull back from investing further ratepayers' money in the facility.[31]

The 1964 proposal from Dublin Corporation's finance committee had been dubbed by the *Irish Independent* as a plan to 'save the Dublin Cattle Market'.[32] However, the signs were ominous when the corporation responded to the call for a review of the market by indicating that no further capital expenditure could be justified on auction rings. As Liam Clare comments, this decision meant 'the writing was on the wall' for the market.[33] Although, sales continued for another seven years, the period from 1964 to 1967 was critical for the market. There may have been an opportunity to reinvent the institution in those years but once this opening was missed, closure was inevitable. In the years that followed sales numbers declined steadily. Between September and November 1967 cattle numbers at the market varied from 2,000 to 2,500 animals. However, by 1969 entries for sales were averaging just 796.[34] To put the size of these sales in context, local marts such as Mallow and Fermoy sold 900 and 600 cattle respectively in the second week of December 1970.[35] In essence, the Dublin Cattle Market had lost its prestige and was now just another livestock sale.

While many sales-masters bitterly resented the corporation's failure to invest in the market and legally opposed moves to close the facility, the local authority's decision was understandable. As we have seen, the market was costing ratepayers substantial sums of money each year in subsidizing its losses.[36] The yearly deficits may also have sapped support for the market, because the tone of much of the council's discussions relating to it through the 1960s suggests that many local representatives were less than enthusiastic about the Prussia Street facility. The local authority questioned the logic of locating a cattle market in a busy urban area. Indeed, as early as 1960 there were calls for the market to be relocated to Dublin Port, while in the same year the council passed a motion calling on the Garda commissioner to 'prohibit and entirely prevent the driving of cattle on the North Circular Road at peak traffic hours'.[37] Congestion was another common complaint, with a motion in 1967 calling for the provision of off-street parking for cattle trucks.[38] It is also difficult to avoid the conclusion that continual efforts by councillors to highlight the extent of the market's losses and overall expenditure on the facility were partly motivated by a desire to terminate Dublin Corporation's involvement in the cattle business.[39] Given the lukewarm support, it is hardly surprising that no clear vision for the development of the market was forthcoming from the council, even though losses were mounting. This was in contrast to the co-ordinated and strategic approach adopted by the market's competition. Mart groups such as Cork Marts – which developed a number of sales centres at Mallow, Mitchelstown, Macroom, Cahir, Dungarvan, Fermoy, Bandon and Skibbereen – and Golden Vale Marts and North Connacht Farmers built up thriving businesses during this period.[40] Divisions among the sales-masters and an unwillingness by the traders to invest in the market also contributed to its demise. Indeed, Clare maintains that the sales-masters declined the opportunity to invest in the market and develop auction rings at the site after Dublin Corporation pulled back from doing so in November 1967.[41] The sales-masters also actively lobbied against the proposed hike in tolls passed by the council in January 1966. Even though the council argued at the time that the increases were essential if the livestock sales operation was to return to a self-financing footing, the Irish Cattle Traders' and Stockowners' Association wrote to the Department of Agriculture protesting against any change in the charges being introduced without the corporation first consulting with the association, 'as was always done in the past'.[42] The failure of the market to move with the times meant the sales-masters' business slowly ebbed away as the cattle numbers declined. The number of active sales-masters fell from forty-eight to twenty-eight in the seven years up to 1971. Ironically, the auction rings also struggled to adapt to the changes in the industry and only Ganlys was still operating in the early 1970s. However, the firm had also bowed to the inevitable and opened Ashbourne Mart in April 1970 with fellow market auctioneering firm Craigies.[43]

If there appears to be a disconnect between the actions of the sales-masters – regarding the increased tolls and their failure to invest in the market – and their desire to keep the Prussia Street facility open, then maybe it was based on the flawed premise that Dublin Corporation was legally required to provide a livestock market. This belief eventually came unstuck in the Supreme Court on 10 May 1973.[44] This was just the final act in a long and protracted process. The physical manifestation of that slow demise was captured by Gerard O'Kelly in 1973, shortly before the market closed. His short film shows many sections of the site cleared, while other parts were derelict, with pens broken down and full of rubble and rubbish.[45] Joe Barry recalled the market's closure as having little effect on the cattle trade. 'It didn't at that point have any huge impact because it was really so seriously in decline.'[46] Jimmy Cosgrave's memory of the market's closing also lacks drama; 'it just died', he said.[47] Ultimately, it was the Dublin Cattle Market's inability to respond to the profound changes in the livestock industry of the 1960s that led to its closure and consigned the Prussia Street facility to history.

4. Dealing for status

What do the oral testimonies, photographs and documentary evidence from the Dublin Cattle Market tell us of rural, and indeed urban, society in the 1960s? As with Cronin's research on the creameries, the testimonies relating to the cattle market give an insight not only into 'workplace, religion and leisure', but also highlight the importance of class and social status in rural society.[1] The fair and market, and later the livestock mart, provided the same social space for the beef farmer as the creamery did for dairy farmer. However, the inner-city location of the Dublin Cattle Market meant themes such as farmer–worker relations and the interaction of urban and rural also arose. There are few references to women or to issues of gender in the interviews but patriarchy is a recurring theme in the oral contributions and in documented interviews. Generally, the oral testimonies complement and confirm evidence from documentary sources regarding the profound changes that were taking place in the Irish livestock industry through the 1960s. However, the personal stories add texture and detail to the broader narrative. In the words of Allessandro Portelli:

> Oral sources tell us not just what people did, but what they wanted to do, what they believed they were doing, and what they now think they did.[2]

In addition, Maura Cronin maintains that oral history can open 'windows' into the past; in this instance, the changing world that was rural Ireland in the 1960s.[3]

Status remained a pervasive force within the farming sector despite the profound changes which the 1960s brought.[4] As we have seen in the previous chapters the demise of the Dublin Cattle Market marked a shift in power and influence in the cattle industry from an elite group of cattle traders and exporters, who had controlled the live trade to Britain for almost a century, to the beef processors and the private and farmer-owned co-operative marts that had come to the fore in the 1960s. However, despite the transformation in the livestock industry, the oral testimonies and documentary evidence confirm that status remained an intrinsic feature of the farming sector and rural society. In her work on the creameries, Cronin maintains the oral testimonies provided 'a lens through which to review social gradation' in rural society.[5] This also holds true for the Dublin Cattle Market. Status and social standing constitute an underlying theme through the various contributions.[6] Cronin observes in her work on class and status that 'a wide gulf separated labourers from farmers'.[7] It could be argued that a similar gulf existed between small farmers and the grazier class who emerged in post-Famine Ireland. The collapse in population and clearance of tenants during and after the Great Famine meant that a pronounced shift from crops to cattle rearing was a feature of Irish agriculture during the second half of the 19th century. As John Feehan states:

> Livestock began to take a firm hold on Irish farms in the years before the Famine, in the decades after the Famine the advance of grazing transformed the face of the country.[8]

It was from these large cattle farmers that the sales-masters came, families such as Joe Barry's, Jimmy Cosgrave's and Raymond Keogh's. The wealth of some of these large beef farmers is clearly evident from the descriptions of the extensive farming and trading interests of the Ward and Keogh families that are outlined in *Strong farmer: the memoirs of Joe Ward* and *Cattleman*.[9] That many of these families viewed themselves as a distinct class and took pride in their connections to other wealthy landowning families is illustrated by Joe Ward's portrayal of a trip to the Ballinasloe Fair:

> Christopher and John brought their best clothes with them on the fly boat and attended functions every night for the whole week of the fair. The Wards were people of good standing in the county, they were educated and they would have met a great many of the gentlemen of similar standing in Ballinasloe.[10]

It is clear that the families who got involved in the Dublin Cattle Market not only saw themselves as cattle finishers but also as cattle traders. Indeed, Joe Barry maintained that the sales-masters' families did not view themselves as farmers but as 'people who traded in livestock' and whose lands were 'warehouses' in which they held cattle. He admitted that in reality the stand-holders in the market were auctioneers 'although they called themselves sales-masters'.[11] The sense that the cattle traders were of a different class to the small farmer or labourer is also apparent from Luke Nugent's recollections of the Dublin market. Nugent was aged 78 when interviewed by Kevin Kearns in 1988–9. He recalled going to the market with his father 'on a good horse' when he was aged 12, and by the time he was 15 he was travelling to fairs buying cattle to sell in Prussia Street. His account of life on the road illustrates the privileged status traders enjoyed and gives an insight into their own self-image: 'We wined and dined on the best, slept in good hotels, [ate] plenty of steak, and you met interesting people'.[12] Although there was a genuine regard and affection for beef producers, the fact that the sales-masters were first and foremost livestock traders is supported by Joe Barry's description of his father's modus operandi when buying cattle. Barry insisted there was a 'strong morality among cattlemen' and that his father always maintained that cattle traders didn't rob anyone unless they were 'fit to be robbed'. Asked to explain that statement, Barry senior told his son that:

> If a man asks you to buy cattle from him and you go into his yard and he shows you cattle and ... if he says to you 'look, I have no idea what these cattle are worth, I'm leaving it entirely up to you and I trust you,' you are duty bound to give him the value of those cattle. But if he takes you on, and he says 'right, how much are you going to give me,' and you'll bid him low naturally and you'll argy bargy; that man you are entitled to rob.[13]

However, Joe fully accepted that the farmers were always at a huge disadvantage when selling cattle since the vast majority of them could not accurately value their stock on a given day because they did not know what the British buyers were willing to pay for them in the Dublin market.

> I remember my father saying that really and truly the cattlemen who operated in the Dublin market ... and he was speaking about his own family – made their fortunes by travelling around Ireland robbing the poor and ignorant. Now it was a bit strong I suppose in one sense, but to a large degree true because you were buying from people who had little access to information. And they were only working on word of mouth as to what to ask for their cattle.[14]

The relationship between sales-masters and drovers also provoked questions of status and class. In many ways the sales-masters' interactions with the drovers was the cattle market's equivalent of the farmer–labourer dynamic. Cronin points out that farmer–labourer interactions were characterized by 'distance and intimacy'; the sales-master–drover relationship was similar.[15] And yet there were clearly differences; the most obvious being that the drovers were predominantly Dubliners and, consequently, did not live in the same locality and community as the sales-masters. However, many drovers tended to work with the same sales-masters over long periods and, as a result, strong personal ties developed between the families. An example of this was the aforementioned McKeevers who were drovers with the Barrys.[16] Joe Barry, Jimmy Cosgrave and Joe Ward were fulsome in their praise and admiration of the drovers as workers.[17] Indeed, Jimmy Cosgrave maintained they were exceptional stockmen.

> They were great men, they were brilliant men with stock and you'd say to yourself what would a Dublin lad know; but they were brilliant, absolutely brilliant. And they knew where to stand, they'd anticipate what way the beast was going and they'd be there, like you know, they were smart.[18]

Equally, the fact that the McKeevers continued to work with the Barrys after the Dublin market had ceased operations confirms the close connection between the two families.[19]

However, Kevin Kearns' interview with Bobby Walsh paints the relationship between some sales-masters and drovers in a more negative light. Bobby Walsh was reared close to the cattle market. He started moving cattle at the age of 7 but was working full-time as a drover by the time he was 10 or 11. 'I was gifted at the game. They said that I was one of the best drovers up there at the cattle market,' he recalled. However, despite being 'gifted', Bobby was usually employed on a casual basis. 'There was only about 20 constant drovers and they lived in a house at the yard … It was mostly casual jobs I done,' he explained. He equated the process of securing casual work to begging:

> It was all a begging job. You had to go up to the corner (Hanlon's Corner) and look for a shilling. Stand there to see if a man would come along with a couple of cattle and say; 'Come here and give me a hand.' And he'd give you a couple of coppers.[20]

In the early 1960s the *Limerick Rural Survey* found that a lack of respect from farmers and the community accelerated the flight of farm workers from the land.[21] Similar grievances were voiced by Bobby Walsh:

> there was no thanks for you, no matter what you done for the men that owned the cattle. Once they paid you a few bob they didn't want to see you till the next time. People would pass you by and wouldn't say hello to you. It annoyed you.

Wages and conditions were another area of contention:

> It was a rough life. You'd no money. It was all pennies and coppers you were working for. You were half starved. Pig's cheek and cabbage and potatoes and corned beef.

However, it was the public perception of the drovers that really hurt:

> A lot of drovers were illiterate, couldn't read or write. They were put down as a very illiterate crowd of people. They wasn't [sic] recognized as much of people at all. But they was [sic] decent, honest, hard-working people.[22]

The experience of Bobby Walsh and the good relations recalled by Joe Barry regarding the McKeevers highlights the variation in working conditions in the Dublin Cattle Market. Writing in the *Limerick Rural Survey* of the early 1960s,

Patrick McNabb questioned whether the poor treatment of farm workers by farmers had been the consequence of their adopting the social outlook of the landlord class the farmers had displaced. He noted that farmers as a class had moved up the social scale rapidly since the 19th century.

> They moved up in opposition to and at the expense of the landlord class. Although firmly excluded from this class, they were to some extent affected by its scale of values, particularly the cult of individualism. Individualism stressed man's obligation to himself and his family. Property was sacred, and man had an absolute right over his property and over his employees. This contributed to a decay in community life and to the harsh treatment of the farm worker.[23]

Walsh's testimony confirms that the need for recognition of status was not solely the preserve of the farmers or the graziers. Furthermore, it supports the contention that the poor self-image of farm workers was a major contributor to the exodus of labour from the sector. Between 1961 and 1971 the numbers working in agriculture fell from 379,000 to 273,000 – a drop of more than 100,000.[24] The *Limerick Rural Survey* blamed the trend, in part, on the poor standing of farm workers. 'The [farm] worker's devaluation of his own occupation has gone so far that he is sometimes ashamed to classify himself as a worker', the survey noted.[25]

The dichotomy of farmers being both workers and employers was also highlighted in the oral evidence. Glimpses of a latent distrust of unionized labour come through in both the testimonies of Joe Barry and Jimmy Cosgrave. The story of Dublin Corporation staff being called to change a light bulb on the cattle stand in the market serves to highlight what Barry perceived as wasteful work practices:

> A single light bulb went, which was the only source of light in the office, and I went to … get a bulb. My father said: 'Don't do any such thing, don't even think of it'. The corporation had to be told that the bulb was gone and eventually three men came down and they spent half an hour changing a light bulb … it was my first example of dealing with, I suppose, the unionized corporation end of it.[26]

Jimmy Cosgrave's assertion in the previous chapter that CIÉ was both inefficient and costly when it came to the transport of stock is a further example of the historic farmer unease with state organizations and strong unions.[27] Cronin points out that many farmers envied 'the ready cash that came from a regular weekly income', despite what she describes as 'their perceived superiority'.[28] The more assertive labour movement of the 1960s was certainly a cause of some concern to farmers. The rising cost of labour in the country's creameries and

5. Some of the buyers and sellers at a sale in one of the private auction rings at Dublin
Cattle Market.

marts was identified in the annual report of ICOS in 1961 as a serious threat to
the businesses and to farmer returns from them. In reference to the creameries it
stated that the 'ever-increasing wage rates' could not be passed on to consumers
because of commodity price agreements and 'could only come out of the
price paid to milk producers'.[29] The ICOS annual report in 1966 stated that a
number of co-operatives had received claims from the unions 'which varied with
locality' but generally sought substantial increases in wages, a five-day working
week, reduced hours and pension schemes.[30] Indeed, Mary Daly points out that
wages rose by 17 per cent between 1960 and 1964.[31] These wage increases were
the source of some resentment among the farm organizations, Ferriter notes, and
led to increased tension between farmers and government.[32] While farm incomes
rose by 20 per cent in 1964, and the agricultural price index by 11 per cent,
the same index had increased by just 2.6 per cent between 1960 and 1963. This
highlighted the extent to which farmers' incomes were subject to the vagaries of
the weather and were at the mercy of export markets.[33] This remains true in the
modern era. As the Cork-based farm consultant Mike Brady observed in 2018,
the two certainties in farming are 'weather variability and price volatility'.[34]

The historic evidence also points to a definite duality in the sales-masters'
sense of status. In a farming and rural context Cronin's assertion that 'land was
the ultimate determinant of social status' in 20th-century Ireland holds true
since the vast majority of the sales-masters had substantial land holdings.[35]
However, in the urban environment of the market the sales-masters had to
prove their worth as traders of livestock, as businessmen. This explains the

6. A farmer and sales-master talk beside the sheep pens during a sale in April 1962.

formal attire of those who worked and traded in the market. This can be seen in figure 5 which shows a selection of farmers and buyers watching the bidding in one of the auction rings in the market in April 1962. An in-depth study of the photographs from the Dublin Cattle Market – such as the 'layered analysis' approach pioneered by George Dowdall and Janet Golden – would undoubtedly prove extremely beneficial.[36] However, even a cursory examination of figure 5 confirms that the attendance at the auction sale was very different to the gathering one might usually expect at a country livestock mart. All of the men are clean shaven and neatly dressed, with many wearing ties and fashionable heavy coats. While five of the men are in soft 'farmers' caps, eight are wearing hats. Virtually all seem to be totally focused on the action in the sales ring, even the two children in the back row – just one buyer appears distracted by the photographer. The same neat dress is evident in figure 6, with the farmer and sales-master dressed in shirts and ties. While there was a tradition of older farmers wearing waistcoats, ties and hats, the dress of those pictured appears to be far more formal.[37] In essence, there is a sense from these photographs that while the market was an interface between the farming and business worlds, it certainly had taken on many of the conventions of the latter. This was totally understandable given that the sales-masters strongest customers were the British buyers; and these were certainly businessmen given the numbers of cattle they traded each week and each year. As Jimmy Cosgrave recalled, some were buying 300 or 400 cattle each Wednesday.[38]

The evidence from the oral testimony also indicates that the notion of status applied not only to individuals but to farm enterprises. Joe Barry attributed his lack of knowledge on dairying to 'snobbery', because beef farmers 'looked down on the dairy man'.

> It was really funny because if a cattleman turned to milking cows he was looked on as a bit of a failure, that he couldn't hack it in the real world so to speak. And, as a result, I grew up knowing little or nothing about dairying.[39]

In addition, it is noteworthy that Jimmy Cosgrave recalled black and white Friesian cattle – which became increasingly popular with dairy farmers in the 1960s – being referred to as 'magpie cattle' when they first appeared at the Dublin Cattle Market.[40] Whether this was just a reference to the colour of both the bird and beast or to the bad luck associated with magpies he did not explain, but it could also be viewed as a negative reflection on dairying. These perceptions could have been informed by regionalism, since dairying was concentrated in Munster and south Ulster primarily, apart from the suppliers of liquid or bottled milk whose farms were generally located on the outskirts of large towns and cities – although there were some inner-city dairy herds in Dublin.[41] In contrast, the rich grasslands of the midlands and east were mainly beef country. However, it is possible that the perceived bias against dairying among beef operators may have been reflective of increased inter-sector rivalry and competition for financial resources from government. As already stated, the extension of the fatstock guarantee scheme to beef from December 1965 represented a major injection of exchequer funds into the cattle industry.[42]

The mid-1960s also saw a significant expansion of the dairy sector as a consequence of higher milk prices that were underpinned by financial supports from government. Total milk output grew from 480 million gallons in 1960 to 775 million gallons in 1970. This was due mainly to higher prices – which rose by 30 per cent between 1964 and 1968 alone – and the realization that dairying offered the best return per acre for small family farms.[43] Indeed, the *National Farm Survey* of 1966–9 found that while dairy farms of between 30 and 40 acres generated an average annual income of £716, drystock farms of 30 to 50 acres had an average income of just £354.[44] In effect, the average profit level on beef farms was half that of dairy units. *Irish Farmers' Journal* editor, Paddy O'Keeffe, attributed the 'meagre' profit margins in drystock farming to a dearth of research into beef breeding and grass utilization on cattle holdings, in addition to fluctuations in cattle prices – which he described as 'among the great uncertainties of Irish life'.[45] With both beef and dairying vying for limited exchequer funding, it was always likely that a certain amount of friction would develop between the two enterprise groups. In her study on the creameries, Cronin contends that farmer camaraderie was 'to some extent superficial' and that farming communities were 'closely-knit but finely stratified' and that 'distinction coexisted and competed with mutuality'.[46] This study of the Dublin

Cattle Market suggests that these observations are equally valid for the farming sector as a whole as they are for relations between individual farmers or within a local farming community.

What was the role of women in the Dublin Cattle Market? Surprisingly, the only reference in the interviews to women at the Prussia Street site related to two nuns who used to collect for charity in the market each week. Joe Barry said the nuns were stalwarts of the sales:

> They were lovely people and they just stood there quietly in their spot in the market and they collected a fortune every week. I presume a lot of it was cattle men salving their consciences by parting with 10s. notes; 10s. was a lot of money in those days, but they would get 10 bob regularly.[47]

The nuns aside, why was there an absence of women in the market? Undoubtedly, the structure of farming in the 1960s was a factor. Traditionally farming, and particularly the buying and selling of crops or livestock, was viewed as a very male-centric activity – although Maura Cronin's work on remembering the creameries confirmed that in certain parts of the country women often did the creamery run.[48] However, the beef industry has always been the realm of the so-called 'alpha male'. This fact is borne out in the various interviews. All of the English cattle buyers were men, the drovers were men, as were the Department of Agriculture officials and the sales-masters. From the interviews, the picture painted is one of a very patriarchal society, with sons being brought into the cattle business but no mention of sisters, mothers, aunts or wives.[49] Interestingly, however, Kevin Kearns' interview with Luke Nugent confirms that women did frequent the market, 'selling pigs or a couple of sheep'. Indeed, he said that women trading in the market would be served drink in the local pubs that had market licences and opened between six and ten o'clock in the morning. However, he indicated that the women had to leave at 10 a.m. 'when there was a proper opening'.[50] Nugent maintained that women more often accompanied their husbands to the market and did the weekly shopping while he sold or bought stock and went for a drink.

> When she had her shopping done, she was never brought into the pub. Never allowed inside. All she could do was put her head inside and say she was finished shopping. And he would say, 'Go out and tackle the pony, yoke it up.' She might have to sit outside there for hours.[51]

This account appears to confirm that the market, like farming generally in the 1960s, was in essence a 'man's world'. Indeed, when placing the cattle market in a modern context, Joe Barry likened its main players to another male-dominated sector, that of the property developer.

But they were brilliant characters all of those cattlemen, they were extraordinary and I suppose in a lot of ways their equivalent today would have been some of the more colourful property developers. They were gamblers and they were men who took big risks, spent money freely and they dealt in stocks and shares a lot as well as in cattle. They were just dealers in every sense of the word.[52]

Conclusion: Going, going, gone!

The 1960s was a transformational decade for Ireland, as rural electrification, group water systems, free secondary education and improved employment opportunities provided by economic expansion totally altered the country.[1] Indeed, veteran rural development campaigner Fr Harry Bohan maintained that on returning to Ireland in 1968 after spending a number of years in Britain he was struck by the extent and the breadth of the changes.

> It [Ireland] had been through four revolutions in a short period. These included the revolution in communications with the arrival of television, the revolution brought about by free education, the changes brought by industrialization and the changes in the church under Vatican II.[2]

A fifth revolution could have been added to the Clare native's list, because, as we have seen, the farming and food processing industry was also in the throes of major change. Cow numbers had increased from 1.2 million head in 1960 to 1.7 million by 1970, beef exports had increased from 48,000 tonnes to 140,000 tonnes in the same period, while, as already noted, the volume of milk produced had grown by close to 30 per cent to 775 million gallons by 1970.[3] However, one of the casualties of this growth and restructuring within the sector was the Dublin Cattle Market. As we have seen, there was no single reason for the closure of the Prussia Street facility; its demise was the result of a combination of factors. The displacement of the fairs by the livestock marts, and the growing influence of the beef processors from the mid-1960s, certainly undermined the commercial viability of the market.[4] Poor governance and a lack of vision on the part of Dublin Corporation, coupled with the unwillingness of the sales-masters to invest in the construction of auction rings specifically for the sale of fat cattle, further weakened the market's influence and importance in a livestock industry that was evolving rapidly.[5] In addition, stringent transport regulations and a shift in government policy to favour the home processing of fat cattle rather than their export contributed to the reduction in livestock numbers at the Dublin Cattle Market.[6]

This study is not solely focussed on the decline and closure of the Dublin market, but, rather, on how its demise highlighted the significant changes in the wider farming industry during the period. Indeed, the development of the mart network, which was a key factor in the Dublin market's closure, can be traced to a greater assertiveness among farm organizations in the mid-1950s and a determination to take on the established interests – namely, the dealers, cattle traders and exporters – who controlled the livestock sales business. ICOS was at the forefront of this movement and records from the period talk of great 'interest and enthusiasm' for the establishment of marts, especially in Waterford, Tipperary, Kilkenny and Cork. An ICOS delegation travelled to Dolgellau in Wales and Melton Mowbray in Leicestershire in November 1955 to 'study the practical workings of livestock sales marts'.[7] However, it was April the following year before the first co-operative livestock mart opened for business in Waterford.[8] The planning and support given at national level to the process of establishing the marts network illustrates the unity of purpose among farmers at the time. More importantly, it demonstrates a determination to challenge vested interests and to embrace radically different, and far better, ways of conducting their business. Daly describes the growth of the farm organizations in the late 1950s and into the 1960s as a 'logical response' to the 'realization that farm prices were increasingly being determined by government'.[9] The success of the mart campaign was a very positive demonstration of what farmers could achieve if they worked and invested in concert. In this sense it was a victory not only for ICOS but for the fledgling farmer representative groups such as the NFA – later to become the Irish Farmers' Association (IFA) – and the ICMSA as it was members of these organizations who generally manned the boards of the new co-operative marts.[10] Indeed, the successful establishment of the marts was an early demonstration of the emerging farm lobby's power.

In contrast, the death of the Dublin Cattle Market signalled the waning influence of the farm sector nationally and, more specifically, it confirmed a serious downgrading of the live cattle export trade. While agriculture was one of the key government departments in the 1950s, and a crucial influencer of national economic policy, its importance as a driver of both employment and exports relative to other sectors had slipped somewhat through the 1960s. There was an acceptance by the second half of the decade that jobs would come from industry rather than from the land.[11] As Lee notes, the *Second Programme for Economic Expansion*, which was due to run from 1964 to 1970, was jettisoned in 1967 because of the limited ability of agriculture 'to act as an engine for growth'. Indeed, as we have seen, total employment in agriculture fell by close to 100,000 between 1960 and 1970.[12] The absence of a rural manufacturing base – with the exception of Bord na Móna and the Irish Sugar Company – which could have provided employment opportunities for those leaving the farm sector exacerbated Ireland's difficulties. This was not the experience in some more developed economies. Haren notes that 20 per cent of the jobs created in the United States in the 1960s were by businesses in entirely rural or partly-rural communities.[13] Despite the farm sector's difficulties, however, agriculture still generated 50 per cent of the state's total exports in 1968 which were valued at £155 million.[14] By 1972, agriculture's share of overall exports had fallen to

42 per cent but had grown in value terms to £257 million.[15] Even so, there was a growing perception that farming was no longer the powerhouse of the Irish economy, and that it was being shifted inexorably from centre-stage to the margins. Jack Barrett, chairman of the Irish Cattle Traders' and Stockowners' Association, articulated the views of many farmers, and possibly non-farmers, when he claimed at their annual general meeting in 1967 that the cattle export trade had been overtaken by tourism in terms of national importance. He told delegates that:

> The premium position of the livestock export trade has been taken over by the tourist trade which got every inducement by means of facilities, advertising and funding paid from public funds, while the cattle trade was completely ignored and neglected.[16]

However, the facts certainly did not tally with this contention. The government had significantly increased its investment in agriculture during the 1960s. Total expenditure rose from £21 million in 1958–9 to £39 million in 1963–4. By 1970 the estimate for the Department of Agriculture was the largest of any government department, with almost half the total expenditure, or £36.5 million, directed at price subsidies.[17] Even so, the sentiments conveyed by Barrett illustrate the extent to which the standing of agriculture – and particularly the live export of cattle – as the bedrock of the economy had been eroded. Was it the relative weakening of agriculture in the economic pecking order that gave Dublin Corporation the freedom to allow the market to stagnate and die through the late 1960s and early 1970s? There is no conclusive answer to this question but it is a view that some sales-masters certainly held.

There are differing opinions on the economic and social importance of the cattle market to the Stoneybatter and Smithfield areas, and of the impact its closing had on the local community. Liam Clare is of the opinion that the consequences of the market's demise have been overstated. He points out that there was 'no local pressure to secure alternative wealth-generating activities in the area'. 'The slow death of the market over many years and its essentially one-day-a-week contribution to the local economy, no doubt lessened its economic impact locally,' he maintains.[18] However, this viewpoint is not shared by Kevin Kearns, who claimed that closure of both the cattle market and the Dublin City Abattoir inflicted a serious psychological blow locally.

> Closure of the cattle market had the most adverse effect, not only because of the economic impact but also due to its psychological status within the community. Since anyone could remember, the cattle market had been the central focus of identity. Virtually everyone had some personal identification with it.[19]

The oral interviews from Stoneybatter recorded by Kearns certainly paint a picture of a community that lived cheek-by-jowl with the market. Maureen Grant recalled being sent up to the market with two billy cans to milk cows that were about to be sold; that was how the family sourced milk. She also explained that on a Thursday some of the butchers in the market would throw cuts of meat 'in a sack' for her mother.[20] Meanwhile, Billy Ennis told of working in the City Arms Hotel and related how the cattle buyers would spend money freely on the day of the sale.[21] In a similar vein, Jimmy Cosgrave recalled the number of farming-related businesses that were located in the vicinity of the cattle market. Auto Cars in Fenian Street were the biggest Ford dealers in Ireland, and the Cosgraves bought tractors off the firm on a number of occasions.

> Lenihans in Capel Street was probably the biggest farm machinery shop for sales in Ireland because the farmers ... they went from the market and maybe bought a tractor or something like that, or a plough or a disc harrow or seed sower.[22]

Generally, the oral testimonies illustrate not only the amount of business that the market drew into Dublin, but they also highlight the extent to which the urban–rural divide was far less pronounced in the 1960s. The market acted as a real interface between country and city, and the stories from the oral testimonies record the banter and craic between and among the various groups. Joe Barry recalled that the wit of the Dubliners was totally different to country people:

> the wonderful thing about the Dublin guys was they added a sharp humour to the whole thing. There was a wit, there was a constant kind of wise-cracking and jokes and having on; they were so quick-witted, the whole lot of them.[23]

However, there were also definite differences. While Jack Donlon said the drovers were 'marvellous fellas', he cautioned that they would 'steal your eyebrows'.[24] It can only be surmised whether the loss of interfaces between urban and rural Ireland, such as the Dublin Cattle Market, contributed to the fractious confrontations that characterized the PAYE versus non-PAYE debates of the late 1970s – which in many ways became areas of contention between farmers and low- and middle-income workers.[25] It would be naive to suggest that the continuation of the Prussia Street sales, and similar urban-rural gatherings, could have eased these tensions; but the loss of such spaces for greater interaction on an ongoing basis certainly did not help matters. Indeed, this is an area that possibly deserves further research; as do the inner-city dairy farms, which were mentioned in the previous chapter.[26]

This study has drawn on a variety of documentary and oral sources, supported by a limited analysis of photographs. As already stated, the oral testimonies have, in the main, complimented the documentary evidence. However, they have also exposed issues that do not appear to have featured prominently in written accounts of the period. For example, the difficulties identified in the transport sector, which Jimmy Cosgrave blamed on a shortage of haulage licences and a perceived bias towards CIÉ.[27] The oral accounts relating to the setting up of the marts were also fascinating and painted a vivid picture of farmer frustration with the fairs and what they saw as the abuse of power on the part of the dealers. However, some of the documentary sources also offered new perspectives on the period, particularly the ICOS annual reports and the minutes of the Irish Cattle Traders' and Stockowners' Association meetings. Moreover, while I have been cognisant of Portelli's warning regarding the 'holiness of writing', I have attempted to give appropriate weight to both oral and documentary evidence throughout.[28]

Much more work remains to be done on the Dublin Cattle Market and its ancillary businesses. Indeed, this study would have benefitted from further interviews, particularly with drovers and Dublin Corporation workers in the market. One of the features noted by Cronin in her work on the creameries was the manner in which 'nostalgia was balanced by realism' in the memories of both farmers and workers.[29] This is also true of the closure of the Dublin Cattle Market. While admitting to loving the bustle of the sale, Joe Barry accepted that the market's day had passed and that the marts were a fairer and more transparent means of selling stock for farmers.

It [the Dublin Cattle Market] was an archaic way of doing business; it was very invaluable for its time but I mean the whole way it operated was for another era.[30]

Glossary of terms

beef factory or beef plant: a slaughter or meat processing facility that is licensed by the Department of Agriculture.

beef cow or suckler cow: a cow from a beef breed, such as Charolais, Hereford or Aberdeen Angus, that are kept to rear beef calves.

bullock or steer: Castrated male animal.

Common Market: 1970s term for EEC.

cull: slaughter or remove animals.

cull cows: old, sick or infertile cows that are slaughtered.

drystock: term used to denote beef cattle or sheep.

drystock farmer: livestock farmer who keeps beef cattle or sheep.

export plant: the same as a beef factory, a slaughter or meat-processing facility that is licensed by the Department of Agriculture.

fat-stock: finished or fattened beef animals that are fit for slaughter.

heifer: female animal that has not yet had a calf – sometimes referred to as a maiden or bulling heifer if she has not been impregnated.

live-exporter or live-shipper: someone involved in the export of live cattle or calves.

steer: same as bullock; castrated male animal.

store animal: one–two year-old beef animal that is not ready for slaughter.

Notes

AFT   An Foras Talúntais
AI   Artificial Insemination
AIFTA   Anglo-Irish Free Trade Agreement (1965)
ATGWU   Amalgamated Transport and General Workers' Union
CAP   Common Agricultural Policy
CBF   Córas Beostoic agus Feola
CIÉ   Córas Iompair Éireann
cwt   Hundred-weight (imperial measure)
EEC   European Economic Community
ESRI   Economic and Social Research Institute
GVM   Golden Vale Marts
IAOS   Irish Agricultural Organisations' Society
ICMSA   Irish Creamery Milk Suppliers' Association
ICOS   Irish Co-operative Organisation Society
IDA   Industrial Development Authority
IFA   Irish Farmers' Association
IMP   Irish Meat Packers
ITGWU   Irish Transport and General Workers' Union
lb   pound weight (imperial measure)
NCF   North Connacht Farmers' Co-operative
NFA   National Farmers' Association
RTÉ   Radió Teilifís Éireann
TB   Tuberculosis

INTRODUCTION: DUBLIN'S CATTLE MASTERS

1 Interview with Jimmy Cosgrave of Enfield, Co. Meath (17 Feb. 2014).
2 Liam Clare, 'The rise and demise of the Dublin Cattle Market', *Dublin Historical Record*, 55 (2002), p. 25.
3 Joe Barry interview (2 Nov. 2013).
4 Clare, 'The rise and demise of the Dublin Cattle Market', p. 30.
5 Joe Barry interview (2 Nov. 2013); Jimmy Cosgrave interview (17 Feb. 2014).
6 Kevin C. Kearns, *Stoneybatter: Dublin's inner urban village* (Dublin, 1989), p. 66.
7 Robert Perks and Alistair Thomson, *The oral history reader* (2nd ed., New York, 2006), p. ix.
8 Kearns, *Stoneybatter*, p. 68.
9 Hugo Slim, Paul Thompson, Olivia Bennett and Nigel Cross, 'Ways of listening' in Perks and Thomson (eds), *The oral history reader*, p. 147.
10 Maura Cronin, 'Remembering the creameries' in Mark McCarthy (ed.), *Ireland's heritages; critical essays on memory and identity* (Aldershot, 2005), pp 169–88, referenced here from the Mary Immaculate College institutional repository and digital archive, pp 4–5.
11 Slim, Thompson, Bennett and Cross, 'Ways of listening', p. 145.
12 Alessandro Portelli, 'What makes oral history different' in Perks and Thomson (eds), *The oral history reader*, p. 34.
13 Cronin, 'Remembering the creameries', p. 3.

1. THE MECHANICS OF THE MARKET

1   *Annual Report of the Minister for Agriculture, 1960–61* (Dublin, 1961), p. 7.
2   Clare, 'The rise and demise of the Dublin Cattle Market', p. 25.
3   Joe Barry interview (2 Nov. 2013).
4   Interview with Jack and Kathleen Donlon of Moydow, Co. Longford (14 Jan. 2014).
5   Clare, 'The rise and demise of the Dublin Cattle Market', pp 12–25.
6   Joe Barry interview (2 Nov. 2013).
7   Clare, 'The rise and demise of the Dublin Cattle Market', pp 12–25.
8   Joe Barry interview (2 Nov. 2013).
9   Bobby Walsh interview as quoted by Kearns in *Stoneybatter*, p. 136; Joe Barry interview (2 Nov. 2013); Jimmy Cosgrave interview (17 Feb. 2014).
10 Joe Barry interview (2 Nov. 2013).
11 Ciaran Buckley and Chris Ward, *Strong farmer: the memoirs of Joe Ward* (Dublin, 2007), p. 114.
12 Michael Schwalbe, 'In search of craft', *Social Psychology Quarterly*, 73:2 (2010), p. 109.
13 Bobby Walsh interview as quoted by Kearns in *Stoneybatter*, p. 138.
14 Jimmy Cosgrave interview (17 Feb. 2014).
15 Bobby Walsh interview as quoted by Kearns in *Stoneybatter*, p. 138.
16 Jack and Kathleen Donlon interview (14 Jan. 2014).
17 Bobby Walsh interview as quoted by Kearns in *Stoneybatter*, pp 135–6.
18 Ibid.
19 Clare, 'The rise and demise of the Dublin Cattle Market', p. 25.
20 Joe Barry interview (2 Nov. 2013).
21 Conversation with Westmeath-based auctioneer, Paul Murtagh (27 Nov. 2020); *Irish Farmers' Journal*, 29 Oct. 1966; interview with a former member of the management team with International Meat Company based in Grand Canal Street, Dublin, who did not wish to be named (interview 9 Aug. 2018).
22 Raymond Keogh, *Cattleman* (Bantry, 2012), p. 66.
23 Central Statistics Office, cattle and beef exports (www.cso.ie) (22 Apr. 2014).
24 Clare, 'The rise and demise of the Dublin Cattle Market', p. 34.
25 Ibid., p. 35.

26 Jimmy Cosgrave interview (17 Feb. 2014).
27 Keogh, *Cattleman*, p. 78.
28 Interview with Gerard O'Kelly of Mount Merrion, Dublin (15 April 2014).
29 Ibid.
30 Jimmy Cosgrave interview (17 Feb. 2014).
31 Joe Barry interview (2 Nov. 2013).
32 Clare, 'The rise and demise of the Dublin Cattle Market', p. 34.
33 *Irish Farmers' Journal*, 7 May 1960.
34 Clare, 'The rise and demise of the Dublin Cattle Market', p. 32.
35 Interview with Micheál O'Brien of Kildimo, Co. Limerick (3 Feb. 2014).
36 Jimmy Cosgrave interview (17 Feb. 2014).
37 Joe Barry interview (2 Nov. 2013).
38 CSO, *Farming since the Famine: Irish farm statistics, 1847–1996* (Dublin, 1997), (cso. ie), cattle and beef exports.
39 *Irish Independent*, 2 May 1970.
40 Clare, 'The rise and demise of the Dublin Cattle Market', p. 30.
41 *Irish Independent*, 2 May 1970.
42 *Irish Press*, 27 Apr. 1971.

2. CHALLENGES AND CHANGES

1   *Annual Report of the Minister for Agriculture and Fisheries, 1968–69* (Dublin, 1969), p. 39; Mary E. Daly, *The first department, a history of the Department of Agriculture* (Dublin, 2002), p. 558.
2   Daly, *The first department*, pp 455–96.
3   Interview with John Shirley (in conjunction with Maurice Colbert) (25 Mar. 2014).
4   Interview with Maurice Colbert (in conjunction with John Shirley) (25 Mar. 2014).
5   Keogh, *Cattleman*, pp 78–9.
6   Joe Barry interview (2 Nov. 2013).
7   Victor C. Uchendu, 'Some principles of haggling in peasant markets', *Economic Development and Cultural Change*, 16:1 (1967), p. 39.
8   Maurice Colbert and John Shirley interview (25 Mar. 2014).
9   *Irish Independent*, 21 Mar. 1963.
10 John Shirley and Maurice Colbert interview (25 Mar. 2014); Raymond Keogh interview (18 June 2014).
11 *Annual Report of the Irish Agricultural Organisations' Society Ltd, 1966* (Dublin, 1967), p. 50.
12 Jimmy Cosgrave interview (17 Feb. 2014).

13 Joe Barry interview (2 Nov. 2013).

14 Maura Cronin, 'Class and status: the evidence of oral history', *Saothar: Journal of the Irish Labour History Society* 32 (2007), p. 36.

15 Interview with Raymond Keogh (18 June 2014).

16 *Annual Report of the Irish Agricultural Organisations' Society Ltd, 1956* (Dublin, 1957), pp 9–10.

17 Minutes of National Farmers' Association's livestock committee meeting on 9 Nov. 1956; *Annual Report of the Irish Agricultural Organisations' Society Ltd, 1956* (Dublin, 1957), pp 9–10.

18 *Limerick Leader*, 12 Aug. 1959; *Evening Echo*, 8 Dec. 1959.

19 Jack and Kathleen Donlon interview (14 Jan. 2014).

20 Portelli, 'What makes oral history different' in Perks and Thomson (eds), *The oral history reader*, p. 37.

21 Minutes of Irish Cattle Traders' and Stockowners' Association meeting on 6 Nov. 1962 (notebook in the possession of Joe Barry, Kilcock, Co. Meath, 2014).

22 Minutes of Irish Cattle Traders' and Stockowners' Association meeting on 12 Sept. 1961.

23 Louis P.F. Smith, Seán Healy, *Farm organisations in Ireland – a century of progress* (Dublin, 1996), pp 68–9.

24 *Annual Report of the Irish Agricultural Organisations' Society Ltd, 1955* (Dublin, 1956), p. 8.

25 *Annual Report of the Irish Agricultural Organisations' Society Ltd, 1956* (Dublin, 1957), p. 8.

26 *Annual Report of the Irish Agricultural Organisations' Society Ltd, 1969* (Dublin, 1970), p. 40.

27 Clare, 'The rise and demise of the Dublin Cattle Market', p. 30.

28 *Annual Report of the Irish Agricultural Organisations' Society Ltd, 1961* (Dublin, 1962), pp 81–2.

29 *Annual Report of the Irish Agricultural Organisations' Society Ltd, 1969* (Dublin, 1970), p. 40.

30 *Irish Farmers' Journal*, 23 May 1964.

31 Ibid.

32 *Minutes of the Municipal Council of City of Dublin, 1965* (Dublin, 1966), p. 66.

33 Joe Barry interview (2 Nov. 2013).

34 CSO, *Farming since the Famine: Irish farm statistics, 1847–1996* (Dublin, 1997), (cso.ie), cattle and beef exports.

35 Estimate based on interviews with Jimmy Cosgrave, Jack Donlon, Raymond Keogh and Joe Barry.

36 CSO, *Farming since the Famine: Irish farm statistics, 1847–1996* (Dublin, 1997), (cso.ie), cattle and beef exports.

37 Jack Donlon interview (14 Jan. 2014); Micheál O'Brien interview (3 Feb. 2014).

38 Jimmy Cosgrave interview (17 Feb. 2014).

39 Maurice Colbert interview (25 Mar. 2014).

40 Clare, 'The rise and demise of the Dublin Cattle Market', p. 26.

41 Daly, *The first department*, p. 352.

42 Ibid., pp 385–6.

43 Clare, 'The rise and demise of the Dublin Cattle Market', p. 26.

44 Daly, *The first department*, p. 353.

45 Off the record comments by dealers and farmers.

46 Daly, *The first department*, p. 469.

47 *Annual Report of the Minister for Agriculture and Fisheries, 1966–67* (Dublin, 1967), pp 39–40; *Report of the Store Cattle Study Group* (Dublin, 1968), p. 33.

48 *Report of the Store Cattle Study Group*, p. 189.

49 *Irish Farmers' Journal*, 13 Feb. 1965.

50 Interview with John Lyons of M.J. Lyons and Sons (15 Aug. 2015).

51 *Annual Report of the Minister for Agriculture and Fisheries, 1966–67*, pp 39–40.

52 *Annual Report of the Minister for Agriculture and Fisheries, 1968–69*, p. 29.

53 Clare, 'The rise and demise of the Dublin Cattle Market', p. 31.

54 *Annual Report of the Minister for Agriculture, 1960–61* (Dublin, 1961), p. 14.

55 Daly, *The first department*, p. 463; John Martin, *The development of modern agriculture, British farming since 1931* (London, 2000), p. 115; H.G. Foster, 'Irish trade with Britain' in I.F. Baillie and S.J. Sheehy (eds), *Irish agriculture in a changing world* (Edinburgh, 1971), p. 74.

56 *Annual Report of the Minister for Agriculture, 1960–61*, pp 7–14.

57 John Shirley and Maurice Colbert interview (25 Mar. 2014).

58 Minutes of Irish Cattle Traders' and Stockowners' Association meeting on 19 Jan. 1965.

59 *Annual Report of the Minister for Agriculture, 1963–64* (Dublin, 1964), pp 38–9.

60 J.J. Lee, *Ireland 1912–1985: politics and society* (Cambridge, 1989), pp 353–4; *A study of the Irish cattle and beef industries*, Economic and Social Research Institute, No. 72 (Dublin 1973), p. 87; *Report of the survey team on the beef, mutton and lamb industries*, Pr. 6993 (Dublin, 1963), p. 55.

61 *A study of the Irish cattle and beef industries*, p. 78.

62 *Annual Report of the Minister for Agriculture and Fisheries, 1967–68*, pp 34–5; *A study of the Irish cattle and beef Industries*, p. 78.

63 *Report of the Store Cattle Study Group*, p. 36 and p. 191.

64 *Annual Report of the Minister for Agriculture and Fisheries, 1968–69*, p. 37; *Irish Farmers' Journal*, 27 Dec. 1969; *Report of the Store Cattle Study Group*, pp 190–1.

65 *A study of the Irish cattle and beef industries*, p. 78; *Annual Report of the Minister for Agriculture and Fisheries, 1976* (Dublin, 1977), p. 41.

66 *Annual Report of the Minister for Agriculture and Fisheries, 1968–69* (Dublin, 1969), p. 37.

67 *Report of the Store Cattle Study Group*, p. 189.

68 Interview with a former member of the management team with International Meat Company based in Grand Canal Street, Dublin who did not wish to be named (interview 9 Aug. 2018); *Irish Independent*, 2 May 1970.

69 Clare, 'The rise and demise of the Dublin Cattle Market', p. 30.

3. NO MARKET RESPONSE

1 *Minutes of the Municipal Council of City of Dublin, 1964* (Dublin, 1965), p. 80; *Minutes of the Municipal Council of City of Dublin, 1965* (Dublin, 1966), pp 65–6.

2 Clare, 'The rise and demise of the Dublin Cattle Market', p. 26; Minutes of Irish Cattle Traders' and Stockowners' Association meeting on 12 Sept. 1961.

3 *Minutes of the Municipal Council of City of Dublin, 1965* (Dublin, 1966), p. 45.

4 Clare, 'The rise and demise of the Dublin Cattle Market', pp 29–30.

5 *Minutes of the Municipal Council of City of Dublin, 1968* (Dublin, 1969), p. 102.

6 *Irish Farmers' Journal*, 23 May 1964.

7 Interview with Joe Barry (2 Nov. 2013); interview with Jimmy Cosgrave (17 Feb. 2014).

8 Jimmy Cosgrave interview (17 Feb. 2014).

9 Clare, 'The rise and demise of the Dublin Cattle Market', p. 25; CSO, *Farming since the Famine: Irish farm statistics 1847–1996* (Dublin, 1997), (cso.ie), cattle and beef exports.

10 Interview with Jack and Kathleen Donlon (14 Jan. 2014); interview with Jimmy Cosgrave (17 Feb. 2014).

11 Interview with Jimmy Cosgrave (17 Feb. 2014).

12 *Irish Press*, 11 Oct. 1967.

13 Interview with Jimmy Cosgrave (17 Feb. 2014).

14 *Irish Farmers' Journal*, 12 Nov. 1966.

15 *Nenagh Guardian*, 1 Dec. 1962.

16 Jack and Kathleen Donlon interview (14 Jan. 2014).

17 *Irish Farmers' Journal*, 6 Jan. 1968.

18 Jack and Kathleen Donlon interview (14 Jan. 2014).

19 Ibid.

20 Joe Barry interview (2 Nov. 2013).

21 Minutes of Irish Cattle Traders' and Stockowners' Association meeting Jan. 1965.

22 Clare, 'The rise and demise of the Dublin Cattle Market', pp 26–32.

23 Ibid.

24 *Irish Independent*, 15 Sept. 1964; Clare, 'The rise and demise of the Dublin Cattle Market', pp 26–30.

25 Clare, 'The rise and demise of the Dublin Cattle Market', pp 26–7.

26 Ibid.

27 *Irish Independent*, 15 Sept. 1964.

28 *Irish Farmers' Journal*, 26 Mar. 1966.

29 *Reports and printed documents of the Corporation of Dublin, January to December 1966* (Dublin, 1967), pp 557–8.

30 *Minutes of the Municipal Council of City of Dublin, 1966* (Dublin, 1967), pp 14–15; Clare, 'The rise and demise of the Dublin Cattle Market', p. 28.

31 Clare, 'The rise and demise of the Dublin Cattle Market', p. 28.

32 *Irish Independent*, 10 June 1964.

33 Clare, 'The rise and demise of the Dublin Cattle Market', p. 28.
34 *Irish Press*, 27 Sept., 30 Nov. 1967; Clare, 'The rise and demise of the Dublin Cattle Market', p. 29.
35 *Irish Farmers' Journal*, 12 Dec. 1970.
36 Joe Barry interview (2 Nov. 2013); Clare, 'The rise and demise of the Dublin Cattle Market', p. 29; *Minutes of the Municipal Council of City of Dublin, 1965* (Dublin, 1966), p. 45.
37 *Minutes of the Municipal Council of City of Dublin, 1960* (Dublin, 1961), p. 34 and p. 261.
38 *Minutes of the Municipal Council of City of Dublin, 1967* (Dublin, 1968), p. 199.
39 *Minutes of the Municipal Council of City of Dublin, 1960*, p. 40; *Minutes of the Municipal Council of City of Dublin, 1964* (Dublin, 1965), p. 80; *Minutes of the Municipal Council of City of Dublin, 1965* (Dublin, 1966), pp 65–6; *Minutes of the Municipal Council of City of Dublin, 1968* (Dublin, 1969), p. 102.
40 Maurice Colbert, *Recollections of the co-op years, a personal account* (Naas, 2007), p. 169; Maurice Colbert and John Shirley interview (25 Mar. 2014).
41 Clare, 'The rise and demise of the Dublin Cattle Market', p. 28.
42 Minutes of Irish Cattle Traders' and Stockowners' Association meeting on 7 Dec. 1965; *Minutes of the Municipal Council of City of Dublin, 1966* (Dublin, 1967), pp 14–15.
43 Clare, 'The rise and demise of the Dublin Cattle Market', p. 29.
44 *Irish Press*, 11 May 1973; *Irish Independent*, 12 May 1973; Clare, 'The rise and demise of the Dublin Cattle Market', p. 30.
45 *The Dublin Cattle Market, 1863–1973*, short film shot by Gerard A. O'Kelly of Dublin Cine Club and produced by Unicorn Films.
46 Joe Barry interview (2 Nov. 2013).
47 Jimmy Cosgrave interview (17 Feb. 2014).

4. DEALING FOR STATUS

1 Cronin, 'Remembering the creameries', p. 2.
2 Portelli, 'What makes oral history different' in Perks and Thompson (eds), *The oral history reader*, p. 36.
3 Cronin, 'Remembering the creameries', p. 2.
4 Joe Barry interview (2 Nov. 2013); Jimmy Cosgrave interview (17 Feb. 2014); Buckley and Ward, *Strong farmer: the memoirs of Joe Ward*, p. 34.
5 Cronin, 'Remembering the creameries', p. 2.
6 Joe Barry interview (2 Nov. 2013); Jimmy Cosgrave interview (17 Feb. 2014); Buckley and Ward, *Strong farmer: the memoirs of Joe Ward*, p. 34.
7 Cronin, 'Class and respectability', p. 34.
8 John Feehan, *Farming in Ireland: history, heritage and environment* (Roscrea, 2003), p. 112.
9 Keogh, *Cattleman*, pp 55–7; Buckley and Ward, *Strong farmer*, pp 32–48.
10 Buckley and Ward, *Strong farmer*, p. 34.
11 Joe Barry interview (2 Nov. 2013).
12 Luke Nugent interview as quoted by Kearns in *Stoneybatter*, pp 141–2.
13 Joe Barry interview (2 Nov. 2013).
14 Ibid.
15 Cronin, 'Class and respectability', p. 35.
16 Joe Barry interview (2 Nov. 2013).
17 Buckley and Ward, *Strong farmer*, p. 114; Jimmy Cosgrave interview (17 Feb. 2014); Joe Barry interview (2 Nov. 2013).
18 Jimmy Cosgrave interview (17 Feb. 2014).
19 Joe Barry interview (2 Nov. 2013).
20 Bobby Walsh interview as quoted by Kearns in *Stoneybatter*, pp 133–8.
21 Patrick McNabb, 'Social structure' in Jeremiah Newman (ed.), *Limerick rural survey* (Tipperary, 1964), pp 205–9.
22 Bobby Walsh interview as quoted by Kearns in *Stoneybatter*, pp 136–8.
23 McNabb, 'Social structure', p. 210.
24 J.J. Lee, *Ireland, 1912–1985: politics and society* (Cambridge, 1989), p. 360.
25 McNabb, 'Social structure', pp 205–9.
26 Joe Barry interview (2 Nov. 2013).
27 Jimmy Cosgrave interview (17 Feb. 2014).
28 Cronin, 'Remembering the creameries', p. 17.
29 *Annual Report of the Irish Agricultural Organisations' Society Ltd, 1961* (Dublin, 1962), p. 9.
30 *Annual Report of the Irish Agricultural Organisations' Society Ltd, 1966* (Dublin, 1967), p. 13.

31 Daly, *The first department*, p. 353.
32 Diarmaid Ferriter, *The transformation of Ireland, 1900–2000* (London, 2004), p. 549.
33 Daly, *The first department*, p. 457.
34 *Irish Independent*, 4 Dec. 2018.
35 Cronin, 'Class and status', p. 34; Joe Barry interview (2 Nov. 2013); Jimmy Cosgrave interview (17 Feb. 2014); Keogh, *Cattleman*, p. 57.
36 George W. Dowdall and Janet L. Golden, 'Photographs as data: an analysis of images from a mental hospital', *Qualitative Sociology*, 12 (1989), pp 183–213.
37 Personal memories of the author growing up in Limerick in the 1970s.
38 Jimmy Cosgrave interview (17 Feb. 2014).
39 Joe Barry interview (2 Nov. 2013).
40 Jimmy Cosgrave interview (17 Feb. 2014).
41 Jack and Kathleen Donlon interview (14 Jan. 2014).
42 *Annual Report of the Minister for Agriculture and Fisheries, 1968–69* (Dublin, 1969), p. 37.
43 Daly, *The first department*, pp 486–91.
44 *National farm survey 1966–69*, Central Statistics Office (Dublin, 1973), p. 118 and p. 124.
45 *Irish Farmers' Journal*, 18 Feb. 1961, 8 Sept. 1962, 18 Jan. 1964.
46 Cronin, 'Remembering the creameries', p. 13.
47 Joe Barry interview (2 Nov. 2013).
48 Cronin, 'Remembering the creameries', pp 17–20.
49 Jack and Kathleen Donlon interview (14 Jan. 2014); Raymond Keogh interview (18 June 2014); Jimmy Cosgrave interview (17 Feb. 2014); Joe Barry interview (2 Nov. 2013).
50 Luke Nugent interview as quoted by Kearns in *Stoneybatter*, p. 143.
51 Ibid.
52 Joe Barry interview (2 Nov. 2013).

CONCLUSION: GOING, GOING, GONE!

1 Lee, *Ireland, 1912–1985*, pp 361–3; Ferriter, *The transformation of Ireland, 1900–2000*, p. 500.
2 *Irish Independent*, 29 July 2014.
3 Daly, *The first department*, pp 483–91; *A study of the Irish cattle and beef industries*, p. 78.
4 Interview with Joe Barry (2 Nov. 2013); interview Jimmy Cosgrave (17 Feb. 2014);

Clare, 'The rise and demise of the Dublin Cattle Market', p. 30.
5 Clare, 'The rise and demise of the Dublin Cattle Market', pp 28–32.
6 John Shirley and Maurice Colbert interview (25 Mar. 2014); Jimmy Cosgrave interview (17 Feb. 2014).
7 *Annual Report of the Irish Agricultural Organisations' Society Ltd, 1955* (Dublin, 1956), pp 7–8.
8 *Annual Report of the Irish Agricultural Organisations' Society Ltd, 1956* (Dublin, 1957), p. 8.
9 Daly, *The first department*, pp 372–3.
10 Interview with former ICOS senior executive Maurice Colbert by phone on 13 Aug. 2014.
11 Ferriter, *The transformation of Ireland, 1900–2000*, p. 549.
12 Lee, *Ireland, 1912–1985*, pp 353–60.
13 Claude C. Haren, 'Rural industrial growth in the 1960s', *American Journal of Agricultural Economics*, 52:3 (1970), p. 431.
14 *Annual Report of the Minister for Agriculture and Fisheries, 1968–69* (Dublin, 1969), p. 23.
15 *Annual Report of the Minister for Agriculture and Fisheries, 1972–73* (Dublin, 1973), p. 15.
16 Minutes of Irish Cattle Traders' and Stockowners' Association meeting on 17 Jan. 1967.
17 Daly, *The first department*, p. 385, p. 498.
18 Clare, 'The rise and demise of the Dublin Cattle Market', pp 32–3.
19 Kearns, *Stoneybatter*, p. 42.
20 Interview with Maureen Grant as quoted by Kearns in *Stoneybatter*, p. 150.
21 Interview with Billy Ennis as quoted by Kearns in *Stoneybatter*, p. 180.
22 Jimmy Cosgrave interview (17 Feb. 2014).
23 Joe Barry interview (2 Nov. 2013).
24 Jack and Kathleen Donlon interview (14 Jan. 2014).
25 Ferriter, *The transformation of Ireland, 1900–2000*, pp 668–9.
26 Jack and Kathleen Donlon interview (14 Jan. 2014).
27 Jimmy Cosgrave interview (17 Feb. 2014).
28 Portelli, 'What makes oral history' in Perks and Thomson (eds), *The oral history reader*, p. 38.
29 Cronin, 'Remembering the creameries', p. 23.
30 Joe Barry interview (2 Nov. 2013).